FORWARD

Several years ago while teaching an Introduction to Theatre course, I found that I was using a combination of materials from several text books plus notes I had been making over many years while teaching the course. It was at that point that I decided to write a book that I could use for both teaching film and theatre appreciation. This book is the culmination of that effort. I need to mention two very important people who shaped my thinking for this book. The first is the dean of all introduction to theatre textbooks, Oscar G. Brockett, and the second is the person who taught me what theatre directing is all about, F. Cowles Strickland. My thinking on theatre, then film, was also greatly influenced by what I read in "The Theatre of the Absurd," by Martin Esslin, the books and plays of Bertolt Brecht, and maybe most importantly Aristotle's "Poetics."

This book is different than most other introduction to theatre or film texts because it takes almost exclusively an analytical approach to understanding and appreciating the theatre arts. It has very little history in it. I think one needs to first understand dramatic structure to appreciate the theatre arts. Later the history can follow. Also, from a far more pragmatic point of view, I think it more fun to start with understanding dramatic structure and enjoying what we watch as an audience or produce as artists. This enjoyment will likely lead to a desire to learn the history of the theatre arts.

Many people have helped me greatly with this book. I must thank several who read this book and functioned as editors, Heidi Burns, Ellen Mansueto, Paula Matuskey and Margaret Roberts. This text became much better because of the notes of these four people. Doug Krentzlin did some very important and tedious research editing for me and compiled the notes at the end of the book. Doh Diago designed the illustrations and formatted the layout of the book. My wife, Melanie Price, was my final visual editor for the book and designed the cover. And finally there are all the students who used the "beta" versions of this text and helped me understand what worked and what needed changing. Thanks to you all.

Perry T. Schwartz
January 2016

Enjoying Theater Arts

Analyzing Theater, Film, and Television

Perry T. Schwartz

Professor, Visual and Performing Arts
Montgomery College, MD Takoma Park/Silver Spring Campus

Doh D. Daiga

Illustration & Layout

Ol' Black Bear Press
Silver Spring MD 20910

www.olblackbear.com

Contents

Part One
The Theory and Analysis

Part Two
The Artistic Side

Chapter 4   Criticism

Chapter 5   The Artists

Part Three
The Business Side

Chapter 6   The Producer

PART ONE

THEORY AND ANALYSIS

Chapter 1

The Basics

Narrative Form

Everybody watches some form of narrative today. We all watch soap operas or weekly prime-time series on television, go to the movies, or attend the theater. All of these events have a narrative element to them. By narrative I mean storytelling. The kind of film or theater or television that involves characters, and doing something of interest to us as an audience in a way that is dramatically fulfilling.

More of us are watching more television, going to more movies, and even attending more live theater than ever before. In fact, we are attending in record numbers. Most of us feel we "Know What We Like"! By the time you finish reading this book you should know *why*. Then because you know why, you'll watch better and better narrative film, television, and theater.

Let's look for a moment at how much we are currently watching. The US is still the leading film box office market with 11 billion in US dollars. China was the second largest market, with a box office revenue of $4.82 billion. The worldwide revenue will grow from $39.1 billion in 2015 to approximately $48 billion in 2019. [1]

The amount of television programming is constantly increasing with cable and satellite television in a majority of the homes in the United States. Most of us own a DVD or download from the internet which has created a video industry that grosses well over $12 billion annually.

Even though the theater has been pronounced dead for many years, the attendance at theaters in New York City and throughout the country is at a record high. In 2015 the League of American Theaters and Producers reported a Broadway gross income of $1,365 billion with over 13 million tickets sold and a "road production" gross of $957 million with over 14 million tickets sold.

This should come as no surprise. Storytelling has been with us since man first began to think. When we look at the history of theater, we see storytelling as central to that theater. The first western theater we know, Greek theater from the fifth century B.C., told stories of kings and queens and gods. These stories were so engrossing and universal that a few can even still be produced today and have an impact on a contemporary audience. Storytelling was central to theater, and theater was central to the Greek audience, who watched comedies such as *Lysistrata* by Aristophanes or tragedies like *Oedipus The King* by Sophocles; it was central to the medieval audience, who watched mystery and miracle plays concerning stories from scripture like *The Second Shepherd's Play*; it was central to the Elizabethan audience who watched plays like *The Spanish Tragedy* by Thomas Kyd and, of course, the many plays by Shakespeare; finally, it was central to the Victorian audience, who became excited by melodrama, cried at sentimentalism, and began to think about the ideas in the plays of Strindberg and Ibsen.

If we look at the time immediately preceding the invention of motion pictures, we would find an audience that attended the theater with as much regularity and enthusiasm as our contemporary audience watches television and goes to the movies. Theaters existed in large numbers in cities, and every town of any size at all had some form of theater or opera house that featured traveling companies performing everything from vaudeville to opera. In an article in The Washington Post, theater critic Joe Brown discusses the planned city concept of the District of Columbia. "L'Enfant would have been gratified to see the highly concentrated theater district that eventually coalesced around Pennsylvania Avenue. During the 30-year period from 1885 to 1915, 37 theaters opened within six square blocks."₂

It is from this narrative-storytelling theater tradition that motion pictures were born and television followed. *Theater is the father, and film and television the children.* As in many family relationships, the children first learned from the father, but as the children matured they became quite different from the father. In fact, the children, because of their success, in many ways forced the father to change, to learn from the children, and in some ways to revert to old ways from the distant past. Let's now turn to a look at some basic similarities and differences between the three media. As has been so wisely said, "the medium is the message." Nowhere is this more true than with the three media that comprise the *narrative theater arts: theater, film, and television.*

Art in Theater Arts

When the term "theater art" is used in this book, it refers inclusively *to narrative theater, film* and *television.* "Narrative theater, film, and television" is simply too much to write over and over again. So, theater art serves as a convenient shorthand. But note that when the terms *theater, film,* or *television* are mentioned separately, only that particular medium is meant at that time.

In order to speak about theater art as art, we must first have a definition of art. The definition that we will use is extremely broad. It is a definition that allows the artist the widest possible spectrum of presentation of ideas, a definition that allows the observer, the audience, the greatest opportunity to open one's mind to as many experiences as possible and think of those experiences as art.

Let us imagine a lovely spring day walking along a street in any city or town we choose to think of. As we walk along observing the trees budding, the tulips blooming, the birds singing, and the joy of people around us experiencing the first warmth and sunshine of the most beautiful of seasons, we notice ahead of us lying in the gutter, covered with rotted leaves and mud, a twisted metal coil from an old refrigerator discarded by some fool who didn't know the proper way to dispose of the remains of a useless, broken household appliance. Most of us would feel annoyed by the intrusion of this ugliness on what otherwise was a beautiful day. But one of us might see something special in this twisted metal. That person might pick it up, take it home, clean it off, put a nail in the wall, and hang it up. Would this old discarded refrigerator coil then be art? That same person might go further and change the shape of the coil, mount it on a wooden background, and put a frame around it. Would it then be art? The answer to both of these questions is, "Yes!" The reason lies in the following definition of art:

> *ART is an intentional expression of one's interpretation of one's environment, expressed through some medium, to an audience of one or more persons.*

Now let's look at our refrigerator coil hanging on the wall. By placing it on the wall it becomes *intentional expression*. Anything an individual experiences and then reflects upon, thinks about, is part of an *interpretation of one's environment*. Therefore, the simple process of picking up the refrigerator coil and seeing it as aesthetically pleasing or even displeasing and putting it on the wall satisfies this aspect of the definition. It is important to presume that the person's *intent* is to call the hanging refrigerator coil--*art*. Fundamental to this concept is that the artist calls a work *art*. In this case, the *medium* in which the art is presented would be broadly considered sculpture or perhaps "found object" sculpture. In this example the *audience* would be the people who came into the room where this art was hanging and observed it. They might all hate it or love it or think it was stupid or brilliantly inventive, but evaluation purposely isn't included in this definition.

This definition is one that permits artists to express themselves freely and permits us, the audience, to experience that expression as openly as possible. The standards of good art versus bad art will emerge as we experience more and as we learn more about the various arts we allow ourselves to experience. This book is designed to give you more information about how the theater arts are put together and to give you a system to analyze them more effectively and thus appreciate them more fully.

The need for a broad definition of art can be demonstrated by the following example. Let us consider the art of painting for a moment. Imagine that there is a person who loves painted pictures of grazing cows in pastures. In fact, he has not seen any painted, framed art other than very true-to-life paintings of cows grazing in pastures. Let's further imagine that he has defined art based on his experience as the following: "art is only a realistic portrayal of cows grazing in pastures." Through some accident this person gets off the farm and into a progressive *7-11* gas station/food store along the road and sees a Picasso print that represents a cow in cubist fragmentation. His response is one of disgust. He sees Picasso's painting as non-art because of his limited definition. In fact he might say, "That's really ugly. Why don't you get a nice picture of a cow to hang there? I don't know much about art, but I know what I like and I don't like that chopped-up thing there." Often what we don't understand or are unwilling to try to understand, we don't like. Just as often this translates into, "That isn't art," because our definition of art isn't broad enough. The point is that as we place limitations on what can be considered "art," we limit what we can experience. This broad definition is used here because it allows us to experience anything that someone calls "art" as "art." We can later judge the effectiveness of that art based on our knowledge and experience with that particular art medium.

Now let us measure theater art against our definition of "art." It might be useful to first break theater art down into its three most basic elements:

> **The Script**
> **The Performance**
> **The Audience**

The Script is written by a *creative artist*. He or she is writing a narrative story based on life experience. This is clearly *an intentional expression of one's environment*. That experience can be triggered by real events or from the imagination. One of America's greatest playwrights, Eugene O'Neil said of ideas for plays: "I don't think any real dramatic stuff is created out of the top of your head. That is, the roots of drama have to be in life, however fine and delicate or symbolic or fanciful the development. I have never written anything which did not come directly or indirectly from some event or impression of my own."[3]

At the point when the writer finishes the script and someone reads it, we have a form of finished art, but not theater art. The finished script is either drama for theater, a screenplay for film, or a teleplay for television. The script is a written form of art to be read, but not until it is performed is it any of the performing arts we call the theater arts.

The Performance of the script by a group of *interpretive artists* fulfills the *expressed through some media* concept of our definition. These interpretive artists and their duties will vary somewhat depending on whether the medium is theater, film, or television, but basically the artists will be directors, actors, and a wide, varied range of designers. The distinction between the writer as a creative artist and the other artists in the theater arts as interpretive artists is an important one. It places the emphasis on the script where it properly belongs. Theater director John Going has stated this quite well: "I've always felt that the playwright is the primary creator and the rest of us-director, actor, designers-are interpretive artists. The playwright is the prime mover and it is his play that we are trying to discover a way to do. One must defer to the playwright; it is his property."[4]

The Audience that watches the play in a live theater performance, in a movie theater, or on television at home thus completes the process. Without that audience we have no theater art. Thus, we as an audience are integral to the process. Our response is critical to the very existence of the art form.

Now that art has been defined and it has been demonstrated that theater art fits into that definition, let's look at our definition of theater art:

> *Theater Arts are the performing arts presented to an audience in either a live theater production, on film or on television by a group of collaborative, interpretive artists working from a script prepared by a creative artist for the purpose of entertaining and/ or instructing the audience.*

The Dual Purpose of Art

Art's dual purposes are *to arouse emotion* and *to stimulate thought* or, as stated in the definition of theater arts, *to entertain* and *to instruct*. However, it is **not** necessary for a work to meet both of these purposes to be considered art. But the artist is trying to accomplish more with the art when attempting to achieve both purposes. As film director Bill Forsyth suggests: "My idea of entertainment would be something that engaged my mind and made me reflect and wonder about things. It wouldn't be switching my brain off, and that's what the cinema tends to do now. You go to the movies nowadays and if it's a comedy, it's like being tickled, isn't it? It's just a kind of motor response. You use comedy in life's darkest situations as a way of shielding yourself. So to use humor to make people laugh without showing them what it shields them from is just using half of the material."[5]

It is generally agreed, when art is meeting both of the purposes contained in the concept of *the dual purpose of art*, it is most effective.

To arouse emotion, to entertain, means to cause some kind of emotional response from the viewer or audience. This means laughter, tears, pity, smiles, disgust, anger, sympathy, aesthetic pleasure; any emotional response. Almost any artist will have some emotional response in mind that he or she hopes the viewer will experience. The goal is that the emotional response the viewer has will be similar to the emotional response the artist intended. If a playwright writes a comedy, he wants the audience to laugh. However, if the audience laughs and feels great sympathy for a character, then perhaps there is more in the play or a particular production of a play than the playwright knew.

To stimulate thought, to instruct, means to make the audience think about some ideas contained within, or stimulated by, the work. Here again, the artist will usually have something in mind. He or she will be trying to state some kind of *thought or theme or idea* through the art.

The *thought of a piece* may be a specific idea about some social issue. Film director Spike Lee's movie, *Do the Right Thing*, is an example. In this movie he deals with racism in America. As with all good art, Lee doesn't supply the answers. He simply raises the questions. Lee does this through characters and situations that are emotionally charged and also stimulate thought. But just so the audience has no doubt at the end of the movie about the question he is raising, Lee juxtaposes two quotes from opposite ends of the *Do the Right Thing* spectrum. One quote is from Martin Luther King, Jr. in which he advocates *peaceful* protest. The other is from Malcolm X and deals with the timing and possible need of *violent* protest. Through this device, Lee is trying to make sure we understand the ideas he is presenting in this film concerning racism in contemporary America.

The *thought or central idea* of a piece might also be a statement about the human condition. Director Rob Reiner's *When Harry Met Sally* is a good example. The film depicts two people who meet in college, become friends but don't particularly like each other, and get together several times over 10 or so years after college. They both go through marriage and divorce, finally realize that they are in love, and end up in a happy marriage. Their relationship is one that the contemporary audience can understand and can relate easily to its humor and pain. Many of us have been there or know someone who has.

In both these examples, the artist endeavors to inspire thought and the understanding of ideas. Playwright Arthur Miller goes even a bit further when he says, "Artists have the obligation to be political."[6] This notion of "being political" raises the question of art and propaganda. First of all let's look at what Webster's *New Collegiate Dictionary* says about propaganda: *Propaganda is the spreading of ideas, information, or rumor for the purpose of helping or injuring an institution, a cause or a person.*[7]

At what point does an idea presented through the theater arts become propaganda? Is any idea presented through the theater arts propaganda? Is propaganda a negative concept? This is critic Paul McComb's idea on the subject: "Perhaps one man's art is another man's propaganda, although we hate to think this. We would like to think that art is something special, and pure, that the artist in the moment of creation plugs directly into what is broadly human, broadly divine. We don't want to think of art as serving any narrow purpose-any merely, for example, political purpose."[8]

But how do we define a "narrow political purpose"? Perhaps the answer lies in the notion that art should ask the questions, not suggest the answers. In terms of "the universality of art," art that will last beyond a certain time period, this is true. Art that deals with a problem that is only contemporary might not be universal enough to survive beyond that contemporary time period.

An example of this would be Henrik Ibsen's play, *Ghosts*. This play deals with the problem of hereditary syphilis, which was a genuine problem in the latter half of the nineteenth century. However, because of the discovery of penicillin, the problem has been eliminated. Thus, the play is likely to seem foolish to today's audience. If Ibsen had made the point that hereditary syphilis was to represent any hereditary disease over the ages, then perhaps this play could be considered to have universal appeal. He didn't, and it doesn't.

The issue of propaganda and art is one in which all of us must develop our own notion of limitations. These limitations should be based on the following:

Art versus Propaganda

1. The intent of the artist and the piece.
2. Raises questions but doesn't supply answers.
3. The universality of the work.
4. The piece allows us to listen to ideas that oppose our own.

In the final analysis, the question of how far can art go in terms of propaganda has a great deal to do with our judgment concerning the quality of the art, how good or bad it is.

Many critics believe if art is to be totally successful, it must accomplish the dual purpose of art. However, the interpretation of what constitutes thought is often varied and broad. The following discussion by critic Alan Kriegsman regarding visual artist Andy Warhol's "Campbell Soup Can" prints is an example of this.

> *When you see those colossal Campbell soup cans on his canvases-and it's very different than seeing reproductions-your mind is blown by the revolutionary character of Warhol's vision, and the uncanny transmutational power of art. Warhol took those things we spend most of our lives looking at, the prosaic furniture of contemporary American civilization-Coke bottles, newspaper cartoons, pictures of movie stars, dollar bills, photographs of violent catastrophes- and allowed us to see them: first, as arrangements of shape and color and line, in this respect no different that our culturally canonized Rembrandts and Rothkos, and in many ways as visually intriguing; and secondly, as disconcerting testimonials to our likes and dislikes, our taste, our values, our leanings.[9]*

Kriegsman tells us these paintings accomplish the dual purpose of art. On the one hand , "shape and color and line" give us aesthetic emotional response. On the other, "disconcerting testimonials to our likes and dislikes, our taste, our values, our leanings" give us ideas to stimulate our thought. We can conclude then that in Kriegsman's opinion Warhol's "Soup Cans" accomplish the dual purpose of art.

When an artist's intention is to stimulate thought, it is our responsibility as an audience to try and understand that thought. We must try to see how the idea the artist is presenting in the piece relates to our society or to each of us individually, or both. Just as we must be open to the emotions the artist wants us to experience, we must allow ourselves to be entertained. We must also seek out an understanding of the thought of the artist, we must try and understand the instruction. When the artist and the audience work together, the dual purpose of art is completely achieved.

Arts Versus Sports

We are a society with vast amounts of leisure time in which we not only do things but also watch things. Some of us, unfortunately, watch far more than we do. However, it is not within the scope of this book to get into the merits of doing more and watching less. Let me simply say that being a "couch potato" is not being an active, effective, audience member. A Canadian media watchdog organization produced the following TV commercial:

> *A young man has a television set for a head. Increasingly frantic, he struggle — and fails to remove it. The frame freezes, and a slogan appears:*
>
> **TV ADDICTION
> North America's #1 Mental Health Problem!**

As viewers, we probably watch only one thing more than we watch the theater arts and that one thing is sports. A individual should be capable of enjoying the ballet one night and a football game the next afternoon. Of course, a set of tennis, a mile run, a round of golf, or a good long walk in the morning between the two would even make one a better audience member and spectator.

Many times we will hear some overzealous sportscaster talk about the "art" of a wide receiver tiptoeing along the sidelines as he stretches out to catch a pass on his fingertips just before he goes out of bounds. There have even been some attempts to compare this activity to ballet. However, the similarity lies in the *craft* of sport and art, not in their basic mission.

The Craft of a Baseball Player

1. To throw and catch a ball.
2. To swing a bat and hit a ball.
3. To run the bases.
4. To understand offensive and defensive strategy.

The Craft of an Actor

1. To speak in a dialect and/or the rhythms of a character.
2. To develop with his voice and body the emotions of the character.
3. To walk, gesture and use facial expressions that create a character.
4. To understand how to analyze a script in order to interpret the character.

Craft means those skills an artist or athlete must have in order to successfully carry out the tasks required of that particular art or sport.

The craft of theater arts and sports involves in many ways the same types of things. Both use the physical and mental capabilities of the participant, but the approach and the outcome are different. One is not better than the other, they are just enormously different.

Though both theater arts and sports have a period of preparation, a plan of action, and a group of observers, the basic terminology and purpose for each varies greatly. The basic purpose of a sport is for someone or some team to win. The basic purpose of theater art is to create characters and situations in which the audience can believe and to achieve one or both of the dual purposes of art: to entertain/arouse emotions and/or to instruct/stimulate thought.

Also fundamentally different is the fact that in a performing art the performers know the outcome because it is planned. They rehearse so that they perform basically the same way at each performance. In a legitimate sporting event the participants do not know the outcome. The following chart compares the various stages of sport and theater art in terms that properly separate these two wonderful observer activities.

One might ask, "Well what about professional wrestling? Isn't that a sport?" Even young children realize the outcome is known well in advance. As a matter of fact, if the outcome is known well in advance and most of what the audience sees is preplanned, then professional wrestling does become a form of theater art, with the purpose of entertaining an audience. It is then no longer a sport because the outcome is known by the participants and to a certain degree the event has been rehearsed. That doesn't mean that professional wrestling is *good* theater art. But since its main purpose is to entertain the audience, it is more art than sport.

Sporting Event *versus*	**Theater Arts**
Practice	Rehearsal
Player	Performer
Spectacle	Performance
Spectator	Audience
Undetermined Outcome	Known Outcome
Rules of the Game	Dramatic Conventions
Spectator Reaction	Audience Response

It is this understanding of the difference between sports and theater art that allows the audience/spectators to enjoy and experience both. We watch sports and theater art differently, respond to each differently, and expect different outcomes from each.

Audience and Believability

Principal to the audience *believing* what it sees in narrative theater arts *are dramatic conventions.* These dramatic conventions are much like the *rules of the game* in a sporting event. In order to truly understand and appreciate a sporting event the spectators must understand the rules. Think of the time you tried to watch a sport you knew nothing about. For most Americans that would probably be the sport of cricket. Watching cricket for any length of time is an effort in frustration if you don't understand the rules. The same is true for theater arts. *There is a set of rules or basic concepts that the audience and the performers agree on in order for the audience to "believe" what it sees.* The rules or basic concepts are called *dramatic conventions.*

Unfortunately, dramatic conventions are not as cut-and-dried as rules for most sporting events. Though there are four *basic* areas of dramatic conventions the details within each area rather constantly change. Also, the basic areas of dramatic conventions are somewhat different for each of the three theater arts; theater, film, and television.

Basic to all dramatic conventions is the notion of *believability.* An audience must believe what it sees in order to be entertained and/or instructed. In other words, the piece must be believable. Basic to believability is the notion of the "world created by the piece." The word *piece* is used to mean play, screenplay, or teleplay, or production of same. Each piece creates its own world of character, setting, dramatic action, and other dramatic and narrative elements to accomplish one or both of the dual purposes of art. This world that is created by the piece may or may not seem very much like our world, like the "real" world.

The problem with the words "real" or "reality" is that our individual realities can be somewhat or enormously different. We each have our own personal perception of what is "real" based on our life experience, our emotional status, and our perspective on a given event. A more precise word is *verisimilitude*, which means *how life-like something is.* A piece can create a world with very little verisimilitude, very little life-likeness, and still be completely believable. George Lucas' film *Star Wars* can be very believable, even though we know the world we see is "A long time ago in a galaxy far, far away" as Lucas says in the opening of the film. Lucas has created a fantasy galaxy filled with adventure and great fun that has little similarity to our own "real" world. If, as we watch this movie, we cannot involve ourselves in this world created by the piece, if we constantly compare it to our "real" world, we will not believe what we see. Then the movie will be a failure because it is not believable. As an audience we must allow ourselves to enter the world created by the piece in order to believe the piece. Any piece can be placed in a relative position on the *Scale of Verisimilitude*. This scale is a bipolar scale that looks like this.

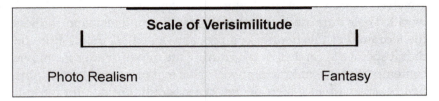

Scale of Verisimilitude

Photo Realism   Fantasy

Photo realism means something that is an absolute duplication of "real" life. A news photograph or minimally edited videotape of an event that actually took place is photo realism. Much of what we see on the news is as close to photo realism as television gets with the exception of live events. Live events, events that the audience sees on television as they happen, do not fall on the scale of verisimilitude since they aren't edited.

Fantasy means an event that is basically created from the mind of the artist. The world created in a fantasy looks and sounds much different from our "real" world. *The Flintstones* and the film *Yellow Submarine* are animation, which is for the most part fantasy. But so are *Star Wars, Monty Python and the Holy Grail* and *Amelie*. They all create worlds that are predominately different from our own.

It is possible for a piece to have very little verisimilitude and yet have a great deal to do with life. In other words, just because the world of the play is a fantasy world or an absurd world, that doesn't mean it can't have a great deal to say to those of us who live in the "real" world. *The dual purpose of art can be met regardless of the relative verisimilitude of the world created by the piece.* Samuel Beckett's plays *Endgame* and *Waiting For Godot* are two excellent examples. They both create worlds that are as much fantasy as *Star Wars*. Yet the significance of these two Beckett plays for a contemporary audience has been written about endlessly. For that matter, *Star Wars* itself has prompted some to ponder the meaning of the obvious good and evil symbols in that thoroughly entertaining piece.

Conversely, if a piece creates a world with a high degree of verisimilitude, it appears to be a very "real" world, it does not necessarily mean that the piece will intend to stimulate thought, to teach us a lesson. The movie *Die Hard* is a good example of this. For the first half of the movie, there is a high degree of verisimilitude. The characters, situation, setting, everything about the movie, look basically like they could exist in the real world. However, by the time we have reached the end of the movie, the *protagonist*, the character actor Bruce Willis plays (the hero), is doing superhuman feats. The relationship to verisimilitude has slipped, but my guess is, for the most part, the audience would still accept this movie as "real" world. The filmmakers have done a good job of setting us up and manipulating us into believing the world they have created, which was based in the "real" world, and corresponds with the "real" world. Their purpose is to entertain us. If you like action thrillers (melodrama) of this nature, you probably loved *Die Hard*. But you didn't spend a great deal of time during the movie or after the movie contemplating the nature of good versus evil presented by this film. Just because it had a high degree of verisimilitude doesn't mean it was anything except very entertaining. That's what the filmmakers had in mind.

Two other elements of *believability* have to do with the audience's ability to pretend along with the piece. The first of these is called, "the willing suspension of disbelief." What this means very simply is that the audience agrees to pretend that what they see is actually happening. Without this concept, an audience would be constantly saying, "This isn't really happening! These are actors pretending to be someone they are not! Why should I believe this?" The other basic element of believability is called "the illusion of the first time". This means that what the audience sees, they are pretending is happening as they see it, as though it was the first and only time it happened. Both the illusion of the first time and the willing suspension of disbelief are basic to an audience believing what they see.

Basic Dramatic Conventions

Four Basic Dramatic Conventions

TIME
PLACE
ACTION
LANGUAGE

Time

The dramatic convention of *time* refers to the sense of the passage of time and to when the piece takes place. The basic rule here is that the time it takes to do things dramatically will often have little relationship to the actual time it would take. *Time will be either condensed or expanded depending on the dramatic needs of the particular scene.* Let's look at a simple scene from almost any cops-and-robber television series. A detective is sitting at his desk and gets a phone call from his partner; his partner needs him in another part of town immediately; he leaves the office, and then arrives in the other part of town. In "real time" this could take 20 minutes to an hour. He'd have to sign out, wait for the elevator, get his car, drive through traffic, and park. In the television series we see him putting the phone down, driving a car down the street with its siren blowing, and jumping out of the car and running up to his partner. All of that would maybe take 10 seconds or less. The audience doesn't want to see the boring detail of "real time." We will believe the condensed time for the sake of the action. Also, for the sake of action we will believe greatly expanded time. In Brian DePalma's film *The Untouchables* there is a wonderful gunfight on a very long series of steps in a railway station, with a baby in a baby carriage caught in the cross fire of a gun battle between the good guys and the bad guys. In "real time" the events in this scene would probably take 15 seconds. The running time of the scene is close to two minutes. We believe it because the action is exciting and our basic concern for "What is going to happen next?" is carried along by this time manipulation.

The audience will also be concerned with the *time period* in which the piece takes place. The basic rule here is that the piece must be consistent with what we know of the time period in history that is presented in the piece. A film about the Middle Ages would not be believable if one of the characters was smoking a cigarette.

Basically all three of the theater arts are similar in the dramatic convention of time. The camera arts might manipulate time a bit more than some very "realistic" theater, but for the most part contemporary theater plays with the dramatic convention of time as much as do television and film.

Place
The dramatic convention of *place* refers to the setting in which the piece takes place. The rule here is that the audience will agree to believe the place as long as it has the degree of verisimilitude the audience has come to expect for each of the three media in the theater arts. The basic difference between the theater and the *camera arts*, film and television, is that the camera arts must look more like the "real" world, and have a higher degree of verisimilitude than theater.

For instance, if a film is depicting a scene at the Washington Monument, the setting the audience sees had better look exactly like the Washington Monument or the audience won't believe it. In fact, most camera arts productions would simply take their camera to the Washington Monument and shoot the scene there, *on location.* That would be simpler than building a set that looked like the Washington Monument.

In theater, the Washington Monument setting would only be suggested. A production might have painted walls that look like marble, benches, flags, a sidewalk, and other things to look very life like, or perhaps just a bench and a flag or two with an actor coming out and saying to another actor, "Well, glad you met me here at the Monument." The audience would then understand the place in its imagination and the play could continue.

As an audience, our experience watching theater and the camera arts has given us different expectations in terms of *the set*. Thus, the dramatic convention of place differs in terms of the amount of detail we expect and the degree of verisimilitude we need in order to believe the piece.

Action

The dramatic convention of *action* refers to the physical and psychological movement of the characters in a piece. The basic rule here is that the audience will believe the action as long as it makes sense within the world created by the piece and is consistent with itself and in terms of the character performing the action. Also, and perhaps more fundamentally, the audience agrees to believe that the action is taking place, even though we know it is not. This concept is critical to believability and, of course, is contained within the notions of *willing suspension of disbelief* and *illusion of the first time*. In order for us to be involved with the "action" we must believe that the villains are actually being killed by the hero or that the two young lovers are actually having their first quarrel.

The major difference between the camera arts and theater here lies in the relationship of the *physical action* to the "real world." The physical action in film and television will generally be much more life like than on stage. Because of the camera angles, the use of different types of shots and editing, a fist-fight or shoot-out will have a higher degree of verisimilitude than will the same type of action on stage. In fact, this type of physical action is more likely to be talked about than seen on stage. If physical action is seen on stage it will be usually of a much shorter duration than physical action in the camera arts. The same can be said for comic physical action. On film we might see a long shot of some "pompous, stuffed shirt" walking toward a banana peel, cut to a close-up of the sole of his shoe hitting the banana peel, and then cut to a medium shot of him on his rear end on the ground looking around to see if anyone saw him in this moment of lost dignity. This sequence of events is designed to make the audience laugh. On stage this action must be carried out in one single movement. That makes it more difficult to do. However, because the audience is not expecting physical action to be as life like on stage as it is on film, they are still likely to laugh.

The *psychological action*, character conflict based on what the character thinks and feels, will be very similar in all the theater arts, with the exception that theater will tend to rely more on words, the language, than will most film or television. Dramatic action will be discussed more thoroughly in Chapter 2.

Language

The dramatic convention of *language* refers to what characters say and how they say it. The basic rule here is that the audience will believe the language as long as it is consistent with what is known about that character. The key here is consistency within the audience's framework of knowledge about a character. An audience would probably have a hard time believing a character who had no education and who spoke in a thick backwoods dialect if he suddenly started philosophizing about the existentialism of man in a manner far beyond the level of sophistication we had been led to believe this character possessed. This would not be consistent with the language we had heard him previously use.

Also in this concept of language we agree to believe that characters will reveal a great deal about themselves and the situation they find themselves in and/or do a great deal in a relatively brief period of time. We not only agree to this but demand it in order that we be entertained. A piece must have language that reveals much about the character and situation and dramatic action that keeps pace with that language. For we, the contemporary audience, have very little patience and are conditioned to theater arts that give us a lot in a relatively short time. That too is a contemporary dramatic convention of which all practitioners of the theater arts are very much aware.

In addition to these four basic dramatic conventions, there are two other important areas of dramatic convention. These two areas are *mode* of the production and *acting style* of the production. Both have a great deal to do with the overall "production style" or manner of presentation of a given piece. For many individual plays, screenplays, or teleplays there are several possible ways or styles in which to present them. This style choice is the basis for the director's interpretation for a given production of a piece. Shakespeare's plays, for instance, have been done in every manner of style, setting them in everything from ancient Greece to Nazi Germany to Shakespeare's time to the future. Style has to do with how the play looks and sounds to the audience as well as the choice of mode and acting style.

Mode has to do with the actors' relationship to the fourth wall or all four walls if the production is in an arena stage. If the actors pretend the fourth wall is there, and don't make any kind of character contact with the audience, it is called *indirect mode*. If the actors break the fourth wall, talk to the audience, it is called *direct mode*. There are very few pieces that use direct mode exclusively. Direct mode tends to be combined with indirect mode in most contemporary theater. The mode of the production will have a great deal to do with its style. If a piece uses direct mode and indirect mode, it will tend to have less verisimilitude than a piece that uses indirect mode exclusively. Until recently, direct mode was predominately seen in theater, but the camera arts have begun to incorporate direct mode in some productions. In some of the films of Woody Allen and Spike Lee, direct mode is used to some extent. The television series, *Moonlighting* and *The Gary Shandling Show*, used direct mode in every episode.

Remember dramatic conventions are continually changing.

Acting style is another dramatic convention. Acting style is determined by the style in which the director or producer interprets the production. Frequently this style choice is inherent in the medium itself. This is particularly true of television. There is a basic style for certain genres presented on television. The audience expects the style of a particular genre. The expected style is a dramatic convention. For instance, there is a Masterpiece Theater style of acting. If we saw that style of acting on *Married With Children*, it would seem unbelievable, because it didn't meet our expectations for that series. For each of the three media, the basic acting style is unique to that medium. There are variations within each basic style, but for the most part television style is different from film style is different from theater style. These style differences are part of the dramatic conventions for each medium.

The various *theatrical forms* have inherent dramatic conventions that one must be aware of to fully appreciate and understand the piece. For example, in musicals one must be willing to accept that characters sing songs and dance to express their emotions, to advance the plot, and to explain the ideas of the piece. If we understand and accept this dramatic convention of musicals, we are more likely to believe the piece. All theatrical forms from straight plays to musicals to opera to Japanese Kabuki theater have their own inherent dramatic conventions.

We rely on these various dramatic conventions as an audience whether we know it or not. If we are aware that these conventions exist, we can guard against becoming too rigid in our expectations. We can let the changes that are constant in dramatic conventions take place and thus open up to new experiences in the theater arts. As actress Kitty Carlise Hart put it so aptly in her autobiography, "The theater has changed, but change is part of the theater."[10]

Television and the Audience

For better or worse, television has become a major part of our lives. We get a great deal of our information and entertainment from television and are watching news, sporting events, and narrative television in ever increasing numbers. We not only have network "broadcast" over-the-air television but also we have cable and satellite, with all its "narrowcast" stations. Plus there are DVD's, DVR's and the internet. All these choices mean that one could watch electronic media every waking hour of one's life and probably not have to see the same thing twice except, of course, for the commercials. It is hoped that none of us will set out to do this. Even the most gargantuan of *couch potatoes* must get up and move sometime, or rot.

Television as one of the theater arts is not news television, talk shows, or sporting events. The television that includes daily afternoon soap operas, prime time fictional weekly series, and made for television movies is *narrative television*.

The individual watching electonic media is likely at home, in a comfortable, familiar chair or sofa, with only one to three other persons. The surroundings are familiar and full of interruptions-bathroom trips, food and drink trips, smart phones, other people talking, and perhaps the most distracting element of all, the remote control. With this device in the hands of the wrong person, the entire 60 to 300 channels on a cable system can be "zapped" or "grazed" through at every commercial break. This does not lead to highly concentrated viewing. Of course, the television industry itself has conditioned us to have a short attention span because of its constant commercial interruptions. As an audience we *expect* to have our train of thought interrupted. It is a *convention* of commercial television. Therefore, narrative television programming is designed to capture and play only to an audience's limited concentration. In terms of the dual purpose of art, this programming is designed primarily to entertain. Most television programs trying to accomplish both the entertainment purpose and the instruction purpose of art will either be on public broadcasting or will be a "made for television special." In other words, for commercial television to get an audience to watch anything other than purely "escapist entertainment television," the audience must be prepared for variance from the norm. There are, of course, a few regular "dramatic series" each season that do *stimulate thought*, currently *Game of Thrones* and *Orange is the New Black* come to mind, but for the most part narrative television is dominated by series that are designed to only arouse emotion, to entertain.

Unfortunately, television's low level of concentration capability can carry over to movie viewing. As an audience, we are in the same environment as "on air" television but are watching a film that was designed to be viewed without interruption, on a large screen, in a large audience. All of this can make a difference in how we experience that movie.

I am not advocating that all the internet and DVDs be done away with. Many times that is the only way to see a movie. Though, with some movies that are designed to take advantage of the spectacular effect of the large rectangular screen, seeing them on

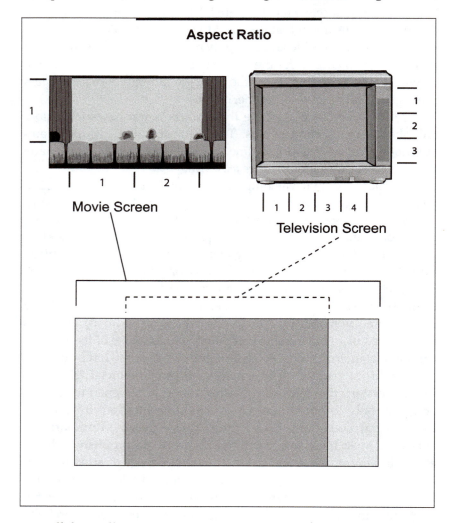

a small, basically square television screen is at the very least a lesser experience, if not pointless. When speaking of the epic film, *Lawrence of Arabia*, one writer said:

In recent years, most people have seen the film in its video version,

*which is an outrage, a disaster. Only the middle or the far left or right
of [director] Lean`s enormous frame survived the transfer to 1.33 to
1 aspect ratio of the TV screen. The cramping would be funny if it
weren't so painful-camels are forever wandering out of sight, bobbing
off into some awful limbo beyond the frame. In one shot-an enormous
vista of desert and sky photographed from up high-the beasts cannot
be seen at all until the last few seconds of the shot, when they push
strangely into the frame from below. Experiencing the movie on video
is the equivalent of lying on the floor of the Hall of Mirrors at Versailles
and watching furniture slide across the marble and out the windows.[11]*

One must realize that some films simply aren't going to transfer to
television very well. A major reason for this is the difference in *aspect
ratio*, the relationship between the width of the screen and the height
of the screen, for television and film.

This has become a non-issue with the introduction of
widescreen, 16 X 9 aspect ratio, television sets. But, if one is viewing
a movie on an iPad or similiar device, the aspect ratio can be an issue.
A smart phone will defintely be a problem but don't watch a movie
on a smart phone. It is just too small!

Let me hasten to add that at certain times all of us need
"escapist entertainment." Commercial television certainly can fulfill
that need. It behooves us as an enlightened audience, however, to
watch the best that commercial television has to offer and not just
mindlessly watch whatever happens to be on.

The audience has an enormous effect on what has been
and what will be developed for television. As an audience, we tell
television producers what we want in primarily two ways. The first
of these is the ratings. A small number of households, around 1300,
are used to determine what the nation is watching. This sample is
randomly selected, and their viewing habits reflect the habits of all
of us. The rating techniques prove to be quite accurate. Considering
the poor quality of the shows that are highly rated, we have much to
do to help develop a more discerning television audience. Each of us
can start by watching only the highest quality television programs.
That doesn't mean that you must watch just "educational" television.
To a degree, all television is educational. As teleplay writer Loring
Mandel said in an article on television:

*Children spend perhaps twice as much time being educated by television
as by school. Television teaches. The problem is, it mostly teaches lies....
The shows teach us that the world is violent but bloodless. That loss, pain
and grief are not consequences of violence. That healing is instantaneous.
That children are smarter than adults. That most women are bleeding
hearts and most men are self-important. That no problem is so great
that it can't be solved in a half-hour. Or an hour. These things are
drummed at us. We hear laughter at words that don't evoke laughter*

and watch anger evoked only by the need for a cliffhanger. We see human relationships built entirely upon false emotions. And we can't easily separate the fantasy from the real.[12]

It is acceptable to watch television that is just designed to be entertaining, but we should try to avoid the kind of television that teaches the kind of lies Mandel talks about. We need to watch television that has high production standards and is honest in its presentation of its material. If we all watch and demand quality television, then commercial television will begin to live up to its potential.

The second basic way we, the audience, influence what is presented to us on commercial television is by what we *buy*. It is called *commercial* television for a reason. If the sponsor of a bad show doesn't sell his product, it will stop sponsoring the bad show, and the bad show will go off the air. Don't buy products that sponsor shows you think are awful! Of course, there is a "Catch 22" here. You won't know what those products are unless you watch the awful show. Also, letters to sponsors and stations that carry shows you don't like are very important. Your letter can make a difference because that station and sponsor assume you represent a large number of people who don't take the time to write. The whole point here is *the audience can have better television if it first knows what is better and then demands it.*

Film and the Audience

When television began to grow in the 1960s and 1970s, many in the film business feared their movie audience would be lost to television. For this reason, many technically interesting films were made, including 3-D films, cinerama films, films with smell-o-vision, and almost anything that a producer could think of that might keep the audience. Though attendance did drop off quite a bit, with 1971 being the low point, the novelty of television gradually wore off.

In 2015 major motion picture studios and independent producers released an all time high of more than 700 films. Movie theater owners had over 40,000 screens in 2015 on which to show these record number films.

Audiences are back at the movies because viewing a film in a movie theater is a different experience than watching at home on television. Couple the more rectangular aspect ratio of film with the large screen and the filmmaker can present us with a spectacular image. It is a spectacular image if we see a warp speed space battle complete with laser missiles as in an action film like *Star Wars* or if we simply see an extreme close-up of someone quietly crying because someone they love has just said a beautiful thing to them.

Filmmakers understand their medium and know that the audience expects spectacular images. The relative width of this image versus its height also gives the audience a panoramic sense, a feeling that the image is surrounding them.

The film experience is also different from the television experience because of the incredible sound systems in movie theaters today. The system engulfs the audience in the sound of the environment of the movie as well as the music and dialogue.

Another major difference between television and film is the presence of an audience. The group effect is undeniable. Think of the times when the response of the rest of the audience heightened your response in a movie, when you were more frightened because many in the audience screamed as a character jumped from behind a door to attack another character or when you applauded as a particular villain finally got his just reward at the end of a thriller. In all likelihood, your response would not be as great if you saw the same film at home on your television or computer screen.

The way the audience affects the film industry is quite simple. If enough of us buy tickets for *Ace Ventura #8*, there will be an *Ace Ventura #9*. So the way to stop bad movies is even simpler than with television. If you dislike a particular type of movie, don't go! If enough of us don't go to *Ace Ventura #8* there won't be a #9. Of course, there is also a "Catch 22" in this basic concept. How can you know you don't like a movie unless you go see it? One could just go to types of films of a certain genre or two. Lets say that you like only "situation comedy" and "melodrama." Then you could simply go to screenings of those two genres. However, limiting oneself to a specific genre is much like the man who limited himself to paintings of realistic grazing cows. Much can be missed when we begin to predetermine what one will like and dislike.

Now let's turn our attention to an increasingly larger problem we have probably all encountered in movie theaters. That problem is the person or group of persons who think they are sitting in the privacy of their home watching television. Because they watch television with so little concentration, they are used to making comments about what they see on television to anyone who is watching with them. They bring this behavior to the movies and annoy everybody else in the theater. The simple fact is if you're talking you can't be an active audience member and effectively attend to the narrative action you're watching and listening to. This holds true for television as well as film and theater. But away from your own living room, you affect others when you talk, and you are then a bad audience member. I was recently in an audience in a movie where the manager of the theater spoke directly to the audience before the movie began. He told us no talking would be allowed, offenders would be given one warning, and the second time an offender would be asked to leave. The entire audience applauded loudly and there was no talking during the film. The following is excerpted from an article by Byron Belt, which appeared in an issue of *Stagebill*. Though it was intended for a theater audience, I feel that it can easily be applied to any audience.

Audience Etiquette

The performing arts season is in full swing. Audiences are set to enjoy the entertainment and inspiration of performing ensembles of every description.

One thing is certain: for many, the performances will be marred by thoughtlessness on the part of too many people who otherwise consider themselves good citizens. These people ignore the simple rules of courtesy, or unconsciously destroy the peaceful environment necessary for enjoyment of many of the wonderful performances being offered a generally eager and appreciative audience.

Here are some rules that should be reprinted in every program book in America. Simple common sense and courtesy will vastly improve the serenity and happiness of sharers in the magic of the arts.

Thou Shalt Not
Talk. The first and greatest commandment. Stay home if you aren't in the mood to give full attention to what is being performed on stage.

Hum, Sing or Tap Fingers or Feet. The musicians don't need your help, and your neighbors need silence. Learn to tap toes quietly within shoes. It saves a lot of annoyance to others, and is excellent exercise to boot.

Rustle Thy Program. Restless readers and page skimmers aren't good listeners and greatly distract those around them.

Crack Thy Gum in Thy Neighbors' Ears. The noise is completely inexcusable and usually unconscious. The sight of otherwise elegant ladies and gentlemen chewing their cud is one of today's most revolting and anti-aesthetic experiences.

Open Cellophane-Wrapped Candies and Cough Drops. Next to talking, this is the most serious offense to auditorium peace. If you have a bad throat, unwrap your throat soothers between acts or musical selections. If caught off guard, open the sweet quickly. Trying to be quiet by opening wrappers slowly only prolongs the torture for everyone around you.

Wear Beeping Electronic Watches or Jangle Thy Jewelry. Owners are usually immune, but the added percussion is disturbing to all.

Snap Open and Close Thy Purse. Leave any purse, opera glasses case or what have you unlatched during the performance.

Sigh with Boredom. If you are in agony–keep it to yourself. Your neighbor just may be in ecstasy–which also should be kept under quiet control.
Read. This is less an antisocial sin than personal deprivation. In ballet or drama it is usually too dark to read, but in concerts it is typical for auditors to read program notes, skim ads and whatever Don't. To listen means just that. Notes should be digested before (or after) the music–not during. It may, however, be better for those around you to read instead of sleeping and snoring.

Arrive Late or Leave Early. It is unfair to artists and the public to demand seating when one is late or to fuss, apply make-up and depart early. Most performances have scheduled times; try to abide by them.
There are other points, of course, and each reader will have a pet peeve we have omitted. However, if just these are obeyed, going to performances would be the joy it was intended to be and we all would emerge more refreshed.[13]

Theater and the Audience

The relationship between the theater and its audience, and television and film and their audiences, differs in three basic ways. These three basic differences are the *live* aspect of theater, the "imagination" aspect of theater, and the physical relationship between the audience and the performers.

The *live* aspect of theater versus film and television is quite obvious. The performers are people experiencing emotions and situations as we watch them, albeit character emotions and rehearsed situations. As an audience, we can sense that humanness, that "liveness," and the performers can sense the audience. The actors can adjust to the reaction of the audience and be stimulated by that reaction. In many ways a really good audience is like the home crowd at a basketball game. That "home crowd" excitement and enthusiasm can encourage a player to set new personal scoring records or block more shots than ever before. By the same token, an audience that is responding enthusiastically to a *good* performance can take the actor to a *great* performance. Communication takes place between the actor and the audience. As critic David Richards says:

'The show must go on.' Indeed, it must. It is all the show can do. Unlike cinema, which stores its treasures in vaults or transfers them to videocassette, the theater's past cannot be preserved. Its dreams

and intuitions and visions take human shape, breathe in the air of the moment--and vanish. The playhouse is the home of the evolving present. The energy generated on a stage encounters the energy emitted by an audience, and out of the collision, theater is born. Or that night's version of it, which may not necessarily be the next night's. We sense that deep down--it is, in fact, precisely what fuels our exhilaration." [14]

The theater demands that the audience use its imagination more than while watching television or film. The theater uses words more than do television or film to create its imagery. The theater will tend to talk more about things and visually show less, or the language of the theater will be more abstract than the language of television and film. The imagery of theater will tend to be more poetic. Also, theater will tend to *represent* rather than *present* an image or setting. For instance, let's imagine a scene in a city park. In a film there would be a real park with grass and trees, birds in the sky, a park bench with two actors sitting and talking on it, a lamppost, a sidewalk with people passing by, and other things that exist in a real *presented*, photographed city park. In theater, we might simply see the two actors sitting on a park bench with a lamppost nearby. This setting would *represent* the park, and the audience would be asked to *imagine* the rest.

Playwright Darrah Cloud talks about the language difference: "People think plays and screenplays are closely related, but they're not. Everything in film is real. Onstage I can get away with red dresses suddenly appearing [on characters]–they're an important symbol. But in a movie, everyone would say, Where'd they come from?....In theater, language can be heightened and poetic. You can't get away with pretty language at all [in movies]." [15]

In some ways watching theater is more difficult and takes more concentration because you must use your imagination more. You must be an active participant in the process. Because of this, the theater experience can involve the audience at a much different level from the film or television experience. Julie Taymor, who designed the costumes and directed the *Lion King* on Broadway says:

That's what's fun about it-finding a simple, theatrical means. And I've noticed that the audience are very happy to see the strings and the rods, [of her puppets] and it pleases them to see the technique. They like to know that it's not all magic, or super technology. We can't compete with the camera, and to try to be so "real" seems a little silly to me. Theater's a medium where you know you're all in the same room, and to see a puppet that's moved by three people and then to forget about the people and see this inanimate object come alive-it's just the most thrilling thing. [16]

The third basic difference lies in the physical relationship between the audience member and the performer. In the theater the distance between each individual audience member and the performers remains constant. If I am sitting in the fourth balcony, no matter how intimate the scene on stage, I will always see the equivalent of an "extreme wide shot." I might psychologically "zoom in" on the performers, but in reality I am seeing all of the stage from a great distance. This is probably not a problem in a spectacle-oriented musical like *Starlight Express* or *Les Miserables* but in an intimate small cast piece like *Driving Miss Daisy* it might be. For this reason, in contemporary theater there are three basic types of theaters that generally house different types of plays.

The first of these, the *proscenium theater,* is the most traditional and generally most common. The proscenium theater is designed with the stage on one end of a rectangular building with a proscenium arch that frames the stage, thereby separating the audience from the performance. The arch allows for a natural barrier between the audience and the performer and easily creates the illusion of the "fourth wall" of the set. In a standard "realistic box set," representing a living room, the audience sees three of the walls of the room and sees through the "imaginary fourth wall" as they watch the play. This type of theater will most likely be the one with several balconies for the audience, have an orchestra pit, have a "fly gallery" to fly scenery–(lift scenery in the air on pipes with ropes and pulleys)– and "wing space," a backstage stage space to store scenery. Most Broadway theaters that feature musicals are proscenium stages. The major advantages of this type of theater are they usually have a large audience seating capacity or "house," it is easier to create the illusion of the real world, and more scenery can be stored on a proscenium stage.

The type of theater that brings the audience closest to the performers is the *arena theater*. In this type of theater, the audience sits entirely around the performance space. The major advantage of the arena is its intimacy and the sense that you are experiencing a live performance. All the technical apparatus of the stage is much more visible, which is desirable for much of contemporary theater. The major disadvantage of the arena stage is its scenic limitations. It is very difficult, if not impossible, to use any kind of walls or backdrops because they would block the view of some audience members.
The third basic type of theater is the *thrust theater*. This theater is a cross between the other two. The audience sits around the stage to some degree. In fact, the most extreme version of the thrust is called three-quarter arena theater. That means that the audience is on three sides of the stage. This type of staging combines the advantages of both of the other two types. The audience is closer than in the proscenium stage, and there also is a space to place scenery since the

audience is only seated around three-quarters or less of the stage. On the thrust stage one gets both the intimacy of the arena stage and some of the scenic capability of the proscenium stage. Tom Szentgyorgyi of the Manhattan Theater Club compares different types of stages this way: "Some audiences feel that seeing a play like *Frankie and Johnny in the Claire de Lune* on a proscenium stage as compared to a thrust stage is like seeing two different plays. In the smaller house it's like sitting on a window ledge listening in on two lovers' conversation. In the larger house, the feeling is more formal, more like watching a play." [17]

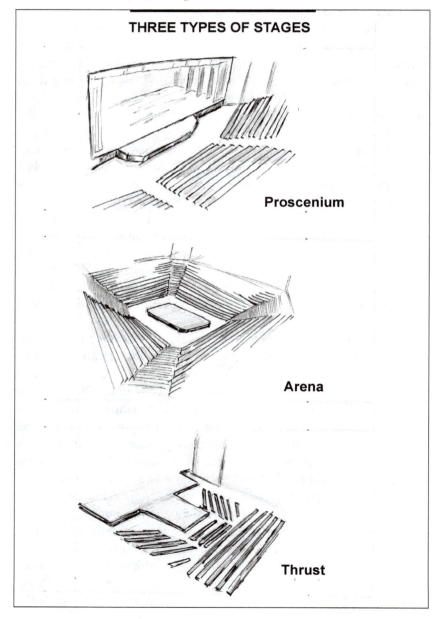

THREE TYPES OF STAGES

Proscenium

Arena

Thrust

Each of these three types of theaters gives the audience a different theatrical experience. These days the proscenium theater is likely to feature musicals that incorporate wonderful spectacle. Thrust and arena theaters are more likely to be doing non-musicals or "straight plays." Audiences determine which of these theaters will survive by attending. So find something you like and go see live theater.

Chapter 2
Elements of Drama

The Poetics

The basis for the analysis used in this book starts with an understanding of the elements of drama as developed in the fourth century B.C. by the Greek philosopher Aristotle. During his life, Artistotle observed the theater of his time and wrote in "The Poetics" what he felt created the best theater. He did not write a set of rules that could not be broken, though "The Poetics" has occasionally through the course of Western theater history been interpreted as rigidly dogmatic. He merely set down observations on the use of the "elements of drama" that he felt generally resulted in excellent theater. These six elements are plot, character, thought, diction or language, spectacle, and music and/or sound. This chapter will look at those six elements of drama from a contemporary point of view. It is a tribute to Aristotle's genius that he so effectively analyzed the theater of 2500 years ago and that his basic analysis still works today.

Plot

When many of us think about a film, a television show or a play, what we often describe to a friend who asks us "What was it about?," is story. Plot and story are not the same thing.

Story *versus* Plot

Story is the basic summary of the events.

Plot is the dramatic arrangement of the events.

Let's look at the story contained in Shakespeare's *Macbeth*. Shakespeare created his story *Macbeth* from two stories in Holinshed's *Chronicles of England, Scotland, and Ireland*. The story is this: two seventeenth-century Scottish generals, Macbeth and Banquo, encounter three witches who prophesy that Macbeth will become Thane of Cawdor and then king, while Banquo will have heirs who will be kings but he will not himself be king. Macbeth is made Thane of Cawdor by the present King Duncan. Macbeth and Lady Macbeth then plot to kill Duncan, and Macbeth becomes king. Macbeth then kills Banquo so he can't father future kings, but Banquo's son escapes.

The witches are again consulted. They tell Macbeth that Banquo's son lives and to beware of Macduff. Macduff, hearing of this, flees to England, but Macbeth kills his wife and children. Lady Macbeth, overcome with guilt because of her hand in the horrible deeds, takes her own life. Macduff returns with an army that overruns Macbeth's army, and Macduff kills Macbeth in battle.

In Shakespeare's play, the plot follows this storyline quite precisely. In fact, for Shakespeare, who usually has a "subplot" or two to go along with the main plot, this play is very straightforward. Shakespeare's focus is on the characters of Macbeth and Lady Macbeth. We get an interesting insight into the psychological makeup of these two main characters who want to achieve power through evil doings. We then see their emotional/psychological struggle to live with that evil. For Macbeth this struggle is revealed by his encounters with the ghosts he sees of the people he's murdered. For Lady Macbeth this struggle is revealed in the famous, "out, out damn spot" scene. The mood of this play is very somber, dark, and tragic. With this play Shakespeare makes a strong statement about the psychological makeup of man.

French "absurdist" playwright Eugene Ionesco in the early 1970s created his version of this same story and called it *Macbett*. In Ionesco's version of the story the witches are much more involved. They not only predict the future, but keep coming back to Macbett and Banco to urge them on. Macbett and Banco are told roughly the same thing about their future by the witches but, they both then scheme to kill Duncan along with Lady Duncan, who after Duncan's death marries Macbett to become Lady Macbett. Through other characters and humorous scenes, the kingdom is portrayed as corrupt and Duncan as a despot. When Macbett replaces Duncan on the throne, because of his own greed and Lady Macbett's urging, he too becomes a despot. The two of them then plot to kill Banco because of the witches' predictions. In the end Lady Macbett turns out to be one of the witches, and Lady Duncan was actually locked up in a dungeon. She emerges and announces Banco had a son through some very odd circumstances. Macol, Banco's son, appears and revenges his father's death by killing Macbett. Macol takes over the throne and promises to be an even worse despot than was Macbett.

The Ionesco version of the story structures the plot entirely differently from the Shakespearean version. It is also written in a much lighter vein. The purpose of the Ionesco version is, however, just as serious. Ionesco has said the following on the issue of comedy and tragedy. "I have called my comedies "anti-plays," or "comic dramas," and my dramas "pseudo-dramas" or "tragic farces," for it seems to me that the comic is tragic, and that tragedy of man is pure derision. The contemporary critical mind takes nothing too seriously or too lightly."[1]

Ionesco's *Macbett* puts its emphasis on the idea of power corrupting. The entire plot structure, as well as the other "elements of drama" in the play, is designed to make this thought clear. Thus, we have two plays based on the same story, with the plots of these two plays being predominately different.

The movie, *Fatal Attraction*, gives us another unique look at this concept of *story versus plot*. The *Fatal Attraction* story is quite simple and can be best understood by looking at the beginning, middle, and end of the story.

Beginning: A married man meets an attractive, seductive single woman. They drink too much and end up in bed together for a one-night stand.

Middle: She wants more. He agrees. She falls in love. He wants out. She turns out to be a maniac and threatens him, his wife, his children, his security, everything in his life.

End: She psychically threatens him and ends up dead. He and his family are back together but shaken.

The plot of the film follows this basic structure through to the end and creates very believable characters. The wife is beautiful and loveable, the children adorable, the husband basically a nice guy who made a big mistake, had a *Fatal Attraction*, and the mistress is a total lunatic but sympathetic to a degree. No good and evil melodrama here, but real characters in a real-life situation. The tension and terror this all creates for an audience is terrific.

Fatal Attraction was originally produced with an ending in which the mistress commits suicide. The director, the producer, and the actress all felt this was justified through character motivation. The film was tested before an audience, and they hated the ending. They didn't feel the mistress had gotten her just dues. A new ending was shot for the film in which the loving wife kills the mistress in the family's bathtub, while the mistress is trying to kill both the husband and the wife. The new ending is perhaps less real but is more shocking than the original ending and audiences felt satisfied with this new ending. What we have in this example is the same story but because of the different endings, two different plots.

Dramatic Action

In *Fatal Attraction* the dramatic action in the new ending created more excitement for the audience and was probably more entertaining, for that reason. During that dramatically heightened ending the predominate dramatic question was, *"What is going to happen next?"* After the excitement of the plot was resolved, the audience could turn to the other basic dramatic question, *"What does this mean?"* Dramatic action, if it is working effectively, can create both of these basic dramatic questions for the audience. If this happens in any piece, it is likely that the dual purpose of art is being met.

Dramatic action in a piece is any activity that keeps an audience interested and creates believability in the world created by the piece. This activity can be **physical/external, psychological/internal, or both.** It can be as exciting as the terror created by *Fatal Attraction*, as intellectually stimulating as the humor and situation of *Macbett*, or as emotionally gripping as the tragedy of *Macbeth*.

If the dramatic action or conflict in the piece is physical–fist fights, gun shots, murders in drama, or running into doorways, slipping on a banana peel, getting a pie in the face, even one-liner jokes in comedy it is external. The conflict happens outside the characters psychological make-up. With physical dramatic action, the basic dramatic question is likely to be "What is going to happen next?" When a plot has these kinds of physical actions or devices that are generated by plot situation we say the plot is *device driven*.

If the dramatic action or conflict in the piece is *psychological*, based on the psychological makeup of the characters or the ideas created by the characters and/or their actions, it is internal. With psychological dramatic action the basic dramatic question is likely to be "What does this mean?" When a plot has action that is generated by the psychological makeup of character we say the plot is *character driven*.

Dramatic action can take on as many forms as there are ideas and emotions. We experience dramatic action through the characters, the situations they are in, the emotions they experience and the ideas they express.

The *central dramatic action* will generally follow through the entire piece, from beginning through middle to end. This central flow of dramatic action is called the "through-line of action" or "spine" or "major motivating force." All the characters and situations in a piece should be tied into this central dramatic action in some way for the piece to have continuity or unity.

If the dramatic action is predominately physical, then the "major motivating force" will lead the audience to the dramatic question, "What is going to happen next?" The piece, in terms of the dual purpose of art, will be designed only to arouse emotions in the audience. If the dramatic action is predominately psychological, then the "major motivating force" will lead the audience to the dramatic question, "What does this mean?" The piece will be designed to accomplish both purposes of art to arouse emotions and stimulate thought in the audience. If the dramatic action is both physical and psychological, then all of the above is happening and we have a very complex, probably more interesting, and maybe the most successful piece of theatre art.

Basic Types of Plot

The two basic types of plot are *linear and episodic*. The *linear plot* in a sense follows a straight line. This straight line primarily has to do with chronology and logic. Generally speaking, a linear plot will deal with time as it would naturally happen. Minutes, hours, days, weeks, months will occur in a "real world" way. Though time will be condensed or expanded, time will not be juggled. Also, any unnatural variance in time will be logically explained in the piece. A character might have a dream, for instance, that would allow for a flashback in time. The linear plot is by far the most common type of plot even in pieces that stray as far in their verisimilitude as *Star Wars*. When a piece has a linear plot the major dramatic question "What is going to happen next?" will be present to some degree. However, this does not preclude the other major dramatic question "What does this mean?" from also being present in the piece.

The *episodic plot* will greatly vary its sense of chronology and usually to some degree its logic. Time will shift in an episodic plot from past to present to future and from illusion to reality with little or no immediate explanation. In episodic plots there will tend to be many scenes, many locations, and many characters, which will seem to be less connected than in a linear plot. Eventually all these elements will fit together, and the audience will ask the basic dramatic question "What does this mean?" more often and sooner in an episodic plot than in a linear plot. The film *Brazil* is a good example of this type of plot structure, as is the film *Pulp Fiction*. In *Pulp Fiction* the three episodes of the film are purposely not presented in chronological order, and characters appear in one segment but not in all segments in some cases. The audience must figure out how the characters and the time relate and what all that means. Episodic plots are far more common in theater than in film. The plays *Mother Courage, The Caucasian Chalk Circle*, and *The Three Penny Opera* by the great German playwright Bertolt Brecht are terrific examples of episodic plots. Most of Shakespeare is episodic, as well as the majority of contemporary plays.

At this point it is important to emphasize that the two basic types of plot are not mutually exclusive. That is to say that one can have elements of the other contained within it. For instance, a predominately linear plot might have some time changes that are not entirely chronological. From the previous definitions of plot, that would suggest an episodic plot. An example of this is the film, *Casualties of War*. In this film, the main character, played by actor Michael J. Fox, is seen riding a bus in what appears to be contemporary time. He sees a Vietnamese woman who causes him to flash back to a time in the character's life when he was a soldier in the war in Vietnam. The remainder of the film follows in very tight chronological order a linear plot that is the center of this tale of men at war. The final scene then takes us back to the bus in the opening scene. Though both the first and last scene are out of chronological order, the plot is still predominately linear, with an element of episodic contained within the entire plot structure. This concept, that categories are not mutually exclusive, is true for most of the categorizing done in this book.

There is a third, somewhat rare, type of plot that must also be mentioned. This type is called *circular plot*. It is cyclic in nature. It tends to start and end at the same place in terms of time. The classic example of the circular plot is Samuel Beckett's, *Waiting for Godot*. In this play, we meet the two main characters just as they are waking up, having slept the night under a barren tree. They spend the day in this same spot waiting for Godot. They talk about Godot, meet two travelers who are passing by and ask about Godot, wonder who Godot is, meet a young boy who has a message from Godot that says they are to continue waiting, and bed down in the same spot and go to sleep. The first act ends. The second act follows precisely the same pattern. At the end of the play, they go to sleep once again in the same place prepared to wait, perhaps, eternally. This is a circular plot. Most examples of this type of plot come from the school of theater that is called "theater of the absurd." This theater emerged in Europe in the 1950s and 1960s as a challenge to the more traditional "realistic" theater of Henrik Ibsen and the "well-made" play, with its linear plot and real life logic. The "absurdists" were taking ideas contained in the existentialist philosophy of Jean-Paul Sartre and Albert Camus and presenting it in a very theatrical way, on stage. Martin Esslin explains the circular plot in the following way in his definitive book *The Theater of the Absurd*.

> *The Theater of the Absurd has renounced arguing about the absurdity of the human condition; it merely presents it in being— that is, in terms of concrete stage images of the absurdity of existence . . . It is striving for an integration between the subject matter and the form . . . Many of the plays of the Theater of the Absurd have a circular structure, ending exactly as they began . . . The relevant question here is not so much what is going to happen next but what is happening? "What does the action of the play represent?" This constitutes a different but by no means less valid, kind of dramatic suspense. Ultimately, a phenomenon like the Theater of the Absurd does not reflect despair or a return to dark irrational forces but expresses modern man's endeavor to come to terms with the world in which he lives. It attempts to make him face up to the human condition*

*as it really is, to free him from illusions that are bound to cause constant maladjustment and disappointment . . . For the dignity of man lies in his ability to face reality in all its senselessness; to accept it freely, without fear, without illusions-and to laugh at it.*₂

In today's theater arts we see little of circular plot and "absurdist theater." Nonetheless, they both have had a great deal of influence in getting us to where we are today, especially in contemporary theater but also in the more thought provoking film and television productions that accomplish the dual purpose of art.

Basic Plot Elements

There are six basic plot elements that occur in most plots whether they are linear, episodic, or circular. These elements are *exposition, inciting incident, complications, climax, major climax, and resolution.* The simplest way to understand these six elements is to look at them in a linear plot structure. For this purpose, I will use the film *Die Hard.* Not only does it follow a basic linear plot structure to the letter but it is also a brilliant example of the genre "melodrama."

Exposition generally is presented in the beginning of a play to give the audience background information about any or all of the following: character, situation, and setting. Effective exposition will supply the audience with only the information needed to understand the "present" situation in the piece. Once this basic exposition is established the plot can start moving forward. Additional exposition will be presented as the plot moves along and more background is needed for new characters or situations as they arise in the piece. In many cases exposition will also establish the *tone* or *mood* of a piece.

In the film *Die Hard* the exposition is presented in a concise, clear manner. Within the first five minutes of the film we meet all of the main "good" characters and understand the basic situation and relationships. The first shot is on a commercial airline, which is landing. The hero, John McClane, is seated next to someone who notices he is gripping his armrest very tightly. The other passenger asks McClane if he's nervous. They joke a bit and a remedy for flight nervousness having to do with curled toes in soft carpet is suggested. This is a "plot plant," which is important to a complication in the plot later. Immediately what we see and hear in the soundtrack and the dialogue establishes current time and strong verisimilitude. Also, we have learned McClane, played by the star of the film, Bruce Willis, doesn't travel much.

As he stands up, a gun is revealed in a shoulder holster. He says to the other traveler, "It's O.K. I'm a cop." And we hear an airport announcement in the background say, "Welcome to L.A. Have a Merry Christmas." Place and time have been established.

McClane leaves the airplane with a huge Teddy Bear, obviously a present for a child, and is greeted by a chauffeur whom McClane wasn't expecting. The chauffeur is a young eager man named Argyle who asks McClane lots of questions as they drive to his destination. From these questions, we learn that McClane and his wife live on opposite coasts. Their two children live with her. He is not happy with the separation or L.A. He's a devoted cop.

They arrive at a huge glass and steel skyscraper. Cut to interior of same where an office party is going on. We meet Mrs. McClane, who is using her maiden name and is second in command in a very successful international business run by the Japanese. We find much of this out while Mrs. McClane is on the phone to her home talking to her housekeeper. Behind her are pictures of herself, the children, and McClane. We also meet a male co-worker of hers who is hot on her sexual trail. She has no interest in this person. Thus we know that she is faithful to a husband from whom she has been separated for six months.

Cut back to McClane coming into the front of the building, he gets security clearance and is told that the party is on the thirtieth floor and those people are all that are in the building. He arrives on the thirtieth floor and is greeted by his wife's Asian boss, Mr. Tatagi, who is very pleasant to him, he meets his wife and they go into her office to talk. They argue over her reasons for leaving New York. She excuses herself to do something at the party, and McClane is left alone to clean up. He removes his shoes to try the relaxation thing suggested in the airplane.

At this point the film has presented us with all the exposition we need. The time, place, situation, and major "good" characters have been introduced. The mood has been established as tense but with a degree of humor. All of this we are to believe is taking place in the "real" world. The plot can now move forward.

The *inciting incident* is the event that begins to move the plot dramatically forward. This event can be character, plot, or thought generated. In the case of melodrama, which is plot oriented, the inciting incident will usually also be exciting and action oriented.

In *Die Hard* a large truck and a car are seen approaching the building. The truck goes down into the parking garage area, and the car pulls up in front of the main entrance. Two men get out. One of them, Karl, walks up to the security man at the front desk and shoots him between the eyes. The second man, the computer villain, starts working on the security computer and tells the rest of the villains in the truck that they are in the building and have taken over the security desk. Out of the back of the truck come about a dozen men and large equipment cases. Several of the villains head off to various parts of the building with the cases, and the others head up to the thirtieth floor. They arrive there in the middle of the party with machine guns firing at the ceiling. They announce their intention of taking over the building and want the head of the company. McClane, alone in the executive bathroom, hears all this and sneaks out to the upper floors, barefoot, to try and call for help. The phone lines are cut just as he begins talking to Argyle in the limo in the parking garage. McClane heads back down to Tatagi's office just in time to see the chief villain, Hans, shoot Tatagi in the head because he won't give Hans the code for the final lock to the safe containing 640 million dollars in negotiable security bonds. McClane is almost discovered but escapes up a stairway. This is the end of the first complication.

The inciting incident is the beginning of the first complication. This complication will involve some sort of dramatic conflict between the opposing forces in the piece. These forces will be plot, character, or thought oriented. Ideally they would be all three, but this only happens in the most masterful of pieces. In the case of Die Hard the arrival of the villians led to the first conflict with the hero. The climax of this complication was killing of Tatagi by Hans and the close escape of the hero, McClane. *The climax in a complication is the most dramatically powerful point within that complication and will come near the end of the complication.* After each climax there will be a slight lowering of tension or dramatic conflict. In the first complication of *Die Hard* McClane has a moment to reflect on the killing he witnessed and try to figure out what to do next. Just as in the total piece, each complication will have its own beginning, middle, and end. Once McClane starts to engage in that next activity, which is to pull a fire alarm, the second complication is under way.

In a melodrama the nature of the dramatic conflict in each complication will be the good guy versus the bad guy. In each complication, the *hero or protagonist* must get closer and closer to being done in by the *villain or antagonist* so that the audience will become ever more concerned for his safety. These complications must build on each other so they become more and more exciting. Of course, the heroine must also get woven into the plot at some point so we can fear for her safety also. In *Die Hard* the heroine, Mrs. McClane, doesn't enter into the clutches of the villain until the last complication.

The *major climax* is the most dramatically interesting point of the play. It is the point at which the various dramatic elements at conflict come to a head or climax. In a character oriented relationship film, the major climax might take place when the two lovers have their final emotional argument that leads to the split up of their relationship. In *Die Hard* the major climax occurs in the eighth complication, almost immediately after the top of the building has been blown off, the FBI gunship helicopter has gone up in flames, and McClane has escaped all this by jumping off the top of the building with a fire hose as a rope. From this explosive climax in complication seven, he stumbles onto villain Hans accompanied by another villain and Mrs. McClane. Emotionally and psychologically this conflict is more powerful than the previous pyrotechnics. Here is the potential death of either the hero or the heroine or both. McClane is forced to throw down his machine gun and raise his hands above his head. He is sure to die. Just as Hans begins to level his gun on McClane, McClane grabs a pistol, that he has conveniently taped to the back of his neck and blows away chief villain Hans and his henchman. The McClanes embrace and head for the front door. All seems well with the world as we head to resolution.

Resolution involves the final tying-up of all the plot lines and dramatic conflict. The resolution returns the situation and characters to a new status quo. In *Die Hard* as the McClanes leave the building they are greeted by Al Powell, who has been McClane's contact through walkie talkie from mid-film. Through their discussions we have learned much about each character and learned to like them both. Importantly, we have learned from Powell that he is a desk cop because he accidently killed a young man when he was a rookie and hasn't fired his gun since. As Powell and McClane embrace, the most vicious of the villains, Karl, whom we've seen in a brutal hand-to-hand battle with McClane in the climax of a previous complication, stumbles out of the building, bloody and seemingly back from the dead. He has a machine gun and it's aimed at McClane's back. He is blasted away by Powell who overcomes his psychological hang-ups to save his new buddy's life. The limo pulls out of the parking garage, dented up after Argyle rammed the villains' getaway van. The McClanes hop in the limo and are off together presumably for a new better relationship, with the villains dead. All is resolved.

These basic plot elements can be most easily identified in a piece that has plot as its primary element of drama. However, these elements can be found in all plots.

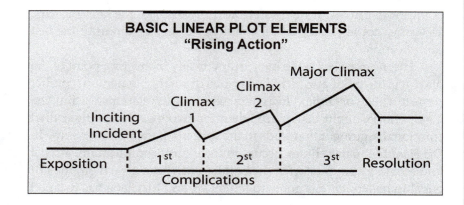

BASIC LINEAR PLOT ELEMENTS
"Rising Action"

Character

Character refers to the "people" portrayed in the *world created by the piece.* Characters can be ducks as in a Donald Duck cartoon, animals, as in *King Kong,* machines, as in *2001: A Space Odyssey,* or human beings, as in *The Eternal Sunshine of the Spotless Mind.* In all of these cases, the characters will have some degree of human qualities so that the audience can identify with them and understand their emotions, thoughts, and actions.

Though characters do not have to always do things that are probable in the "real world," we do expect them to do things that are credible in the world created by the piece. In the film *Superman: The Movie* we are not surprised to see the main character fly and do things because of his superhuman strength. We accept these "unreal" activities because the film tells us that Superman is from another planet and gives us a quasi-scientific explanation for his powers. Therefore, the character of Superman is credible within "the world created by the piece."

Characters must also be *consistent* within themselves and the world created by the piece. Superman constantly does good deeds. If all of a sudden he kicked a dog into the path of an oncoming truck, we would be stunned. In fact, we would probably stop believing the film, and say to ourselves, "Superman wouldn't do something like that!" That action would not be consistent with the other actions we had seen the character do.

A way to analyze characters at the most basic level is to look at how completely a character is developed psychologically. *Psychological character development or character traits are referred to in terms of dimensional complexity or degree of development.* In these terms a character is called *one-dimensional* if he or she has only a few psychological character traits revealed to an audience. The characters in the film *Die Hard* are one-dimensional. Each character is basically good or evil, and we know little beyond that about them psychologically. Generally speaking, a piece with one-dimensional characters will be heavily *plot oriented.* A character is called *multi-dimensional* if the character has many psychological character traits revealed to an audience. The characters in the play *Equus* are very complex psychologically. In fact, part of the enjoyment of a play/film like *Driving Miss Daisy* is for the audience to try to understand the complex psychological make-up of the characters. Generally speaking, a play with multi-dimensional characters will be *character and/or thought oriented.*

A character will be revealed to the audience in several different ways called "aspects of character." The first aspect of character has to do with the *psychological/emotional make-up* of the character. This concept includes the *degree of development of character* as well as the degree of change in character throughout the piece. This degree of change is referred to as "psychological/emotional character growth." Even in a film with one-dimensional characters the degree of change is important. In *Die Hard* we see the McClanes, hero and heroine, make a basic psychological/emotional change. They realize after their brush with death that they are important to each other and they should be together. This is very simplistic and romanticized, but in keeping with the characters, and it is a change. In a piece with multi-dimensional characters the changes will be more complex, more thought provoking and not so obvious. In *Driving Miss Daisy*, Miss Daisy and her chauffeur realize how important they are to each other in spite of the differences in social status and race. The audience has seen this develop through the piece as these very complex characters interact with each other.

The second aspect of character has to do with the *physical appearance* of the character. The character's body and face, along with the clothes the character wears, have a great impact on the audience. A Superman who was short, flabby, unshaven, and cross-eyed flying around in a rumpled business suit would just not have the same effect on the audience as Christopher Reeve does in his cape and tights. The audience judges a character to a great degree on how a character looks. In the film *Pretty Woman*, the female lead, Vivian, is a hooker. In the beginning of the film she looks every bit the hooker from her walk to her short skirt to her too-red lipstick. When she is hired by the leading man to be his escort for a week, he gives her money to buy new clothes so she will be acceptable in the business world. With the elegant but sexy new clothes, she is a new woman, a "pretty woman," and no longer a hooker. Her walk even changes. Psychologically, she is the same character. But the clothes and her physical changes in mannerism make her different.

The *verbal element of character* is the third aspect. Obviously what we hear in terms of dialogue is principal to the theater arts. *Characters are revealed to us by what they say and what others say about them.* We learn much about a character if what he says about himself is similar or different than what others say about him. Also, we learn much about a character if her actions reinforce or contradict her words.

The *character's actions* or what a character does is the fourth aspect of character. The actions of a character also reveal a great deal about that character. *If the actions of a character contradict his words, the audience will believe the action as the true character trait.* When the villain Hans in *Die Hard* says, "We mean no one harm," and then proceeds to shoot Tatagi in the head in the next scene, we realize his actions reveal the true character trait. Actions in characters, as in life, speak louder than words.

Thought

When a piece accomplishes the dual purpose of art, the thought that is stimulated or instruction that takes place happens to a great degree because thought is more or less emphasized in the piece. *Thought is the main theme or idea or message* that the audience takes away from the piece and thinks about or talks about. It's important to remember that for the most part, in terms of thought, the theater arts should only raise questions and not supply answers. When the answers are too specifically given, the art approaches the area of propaganda, which has been discussed in Chapter 1.

The thought generally will cover one of two basic areas: social ideas or psychological/emotional ideas. In some cases the thought will incorporate both of these basic areas. The film *Fatal Attraction* presented a major thought that dealt with both the social idea of infidelity in male/female relationships and the psychological/emotional idea of a mentally unstable person who creates havoc in a marriage because of a relationship with one of the partners in that marriage. These were ideas to which the audience could relate and talk about after being thoroughly entertained by an exciting film. In a society where promiscuity is common, even in marriages, is there such a thing as a "safe" sexual encounter? Was the instability of "the other woman" caused by the relationship, or was she that way prior to the relationship? How can anyone know the potential of that kind of "madness" in another person before the demon is unleashed and it's too late? These are the kind of social and psychological/emotional questions that an effective, thought-oriented piece can generate.

Generally speaking, a piece that is effectively written in terms of thought will not just come out and tell the audience what the author is trying to say. In a sense effective writing is something like a puzzle. Solving that puzzle is part of the enjoyment of the theater arts for an audience. The author gives us many clues as the piece unfolds which are sections of the puzzle. These clues are usually contained in the title, the characters, the plot and in the symbols and/or allegories the author uses.

The *title* will often be the first place the piece presents a clue to the main thought or idea. Henrik Ibsen's masterpiece of psychological realism, *A Doll's House*, is a good example of this. The thought of this play has to do with a woman being treated as an equal in a marriage.

In the late 1800s, when the play was written and produced, this concept caused a riot in the theater. Nora, the main female character, is treated like a "doll" by her husband, Torvald, and is given no responsibility of any sort in the marriage. She symbolically lived in a "doll's house." In this case the title is used to represent the main idea or thought of the play.

The *characters*, Nora and Torvald, present the two sides of the issue that Ibsen dramatizes. Nora is a woman who feels stifled by the "doll-like" treatment of her husband and all the other men around her. Torvald isn't even aware of her unhappiness. He simply assumes that because she is a woman she is happy to be treated the way all women were treated in the nineteenth century in Europe. In fact, he can't imagine she couldn't be happy as she lives in a grand house, wanting for nothing, with no worries, and none of the obligations of a man. All of these ideas, this thought, the audience understands *through characterization*.

In *A Doll's House* the plot also reinforces the thought. Nora borrows money to solve a financial problem but must forge her husband's signature to do it. Women couldn't borrow money at the time. This ends up in a scandal, and she leaves her home rather than stay in the suffocating doll's house. *The plot* can help make the thought understandable.

A *symbol* is a device that concretely represents an idea. The two main characters in *A Doll's House* are symbols of the two different sides of the issue of women's rights. Characters will often symbolize some aspect of the thought of the piece. In fact, almost any element of a production can serve as a symbol to convey the ideas of that production. The difficulty in presenting symbols to an audience is in walking the fine line between being too obvious versus being too obscure. Part of the mental enjoyment for an audience is being able to work at interpreting and understanding the symbols in the production. The symbols, too, are pieces in the puzzle of thought.

The use of *allegory* can also contribute to thought. *An allegory personifies an abstract quality or idea.* In Wim Wender's film, *Wings of Desire*, the abstract notion of angels is personified in the form of middle-aged men in long overcoats with neck scarves and wrinkled business suits who follow people around listening to their thoughts. This is not only a unique personification but takes a fair amount of the film to understand. This forces the audience to deal from the beginning of the film with the dramatic question, "What does this mean?" With the use of this complex and puzzling allegory the filmmaker is signaling to the audience that this is a film centered on thought.

45

Diction

Diction refers to the *language* of the piece. The diction is presented to the audience through dialogue or narration. The basic rule concerning diction and character is that the language must match the character's education, temperament, regionalism, or nationality, and other basic aspects of a character's background and make-up. If a character is supposed to be uneducated and from the Bronx, then the audience would have some trouble believing in her if her sentence structure is grammatically correct. It would be even worse if that same character slipped in and out of a Bronx regional dialect. These are considerations of diction.

Even though metered poetry is rarely written for the theater arts these days, *imagery* is still very important. Imagery has to do with the manner in which the author structures the dialogue of the characters, the mood or tone created by the images presented in that dialogue, and the types of metaphors, similes, and other types of comparative devices as well as the use of symbols and allegories by the writer.

In Charles Fuller's *A Soldier's Play*, concerning racism in America, listen to the poetic imagery in this dialogue from the character C. J., whom another main character, Waters, describes as a person who "just smiles, can't talk, barely read or write his own name.

> . . . You remember I tol' you 'bout a place I use ta go outside Carmella? When I was a little ole tiny thing? Place out behind O'Connell's farm? Place would be stinkin' of plums, Cobb. Shaded-that ripe smell be weavin' through the cotton fields and clear on in ta town on a warm day. First time I had Evelyn? I had her unda' them plum trees. I wrote a song for her-(talks, sings) My ginger-colored Moma-she had thighs the size of hams! (chuckles) And when you spread them Momaaaaa! (talks) You let me have my jelly roll and jam! (Pause, mood swing) O'Connell, he had a dog-meanes' dog I eva' see! An' the only way you could enjoy them plum trees was to outsmart that dog. Waters is like that ole dog, Cobb-you hadta' run circles roun' ol' Windy-that was his name. They say he tore a man's arm off once, and got to likin' it. So, you had to cheat that dog outta' bitin' you every time. Every time[3]

The ideas suggested in this speech are that of an intelligent person and might seem too sophisticated for this character. But the language playwright Fuller has this character speak is full of colorful, meaningful, poetic imagery that sounds entirely believable in this play.

The writer must reveal a great deal about character, plot, and thought in a very short time span through diction. *The keys to effective diction are believable language, dramatically interesting language, and language that is concise and vivid in its imagery.*

Spectacle

Spectacle refers to *everything that is visual* in a piece. This means the costumes, sets, lighting, make-up, props, special effects, and anything else that the audience sees in a piece. In film and television the movement of the camera is an aspect of spectacle. The movement of the actors can also be considered an aspect of spectacle.

When spectacle is emphasized, the spectacle in the piece would in some way be *special or spectacular*. In a "period" piece like Christopher Hampton's *Dangerous Liaisons* which is set in eighteenth-century France, the costumes, sets, props, and lighting were all done to give a look of historical accuracy. The spectacle of the piece enhanced the overall effect. Because the aristocrats portrayed lived in a society that looked so much different from our own, as an audience we could maintain a certain objective distance to the characters. For that reason, perhaps we could better understand the danger in the liaisons we were watching unfold and then perhaps relate them to our own lives and society. The historical spectacle was important to this piece because it was entertaining and helps the audience understand the thought of the piece.

Star Wars gives us another type of spectacle in the fantasy world that director George Lucas creates. This world is not only peopled with "fantasy creatures" but also presents us with special battle effects that are truly spectacular and graphically fantastic. In this film, Lucas sets the audience up at the very beginning explaining that the story we are about to see happens in "a long time ago in a galaxy far, far away." What this means to us is that we are about to enter a world created in the director's imagination, a fantasy world filled with delightful, high adventure spectacle.

The film *Alien* also relies on special effects to create some of its spectacle. But unlike *Star Wars*, *Alien* tries to create a world that is futuristic but plausible based on the audience's understanding of current science. The giant spaceship we see looks the way the inside of a huge oil tanker in space might look. Most of the characters in the film are complex human beings. The lighting, sets, and costumes seem imaginable in an outer space future. Even the *Alien* monster seems life-like. The explanation for the monster has a basis in some sense of scientific logic. Therefore, though spectacle is very important in *Alien* as it is in *Star Wars, Alien* is science fiction, and *Star Wars* is fantasy. In any performance from the most "life-like" to the most bizarre fantasy, effective spectacle will help us believe the world created by the piece.

It is important to note that while some pieces *emphasize* spectacle, *all* films, television, and theater have an element of spectacle in them. We see sets, costumes, lighting, and other visual elements in everything we see as a theater art.

Music and Sound

Music refers to any type of music that is used in a piece from *background music to songs* that are sung and played by the performers of the piece. The most common type of music, is background music, which is most often used to help *establish or reinforce mood*. The television series, *NYPD Blue,* is a good example. The use of Japanese Koto drums in the theme music creates a sense of tension that is reflected in the overall mood of the piece. Ideally the background music should be so effectively incorporated into the piece, should be so "unified" with the other elements of drama, that the audience doesn't even notice it.

Sound refers to all the background audio that is used in film and television, and now more and more in theater, to help the audience have a sense of the environment in which the piece takes place. In many cases these sounds are "scored" in the same sense that music is scored. Environmental sounds can be more complex than background music and sometimes even replace it in a film. The terrified breathing inside her space helmet as the heroine in Alien makes her final attempt to get rid of the monster, the sounds of spaceship engines and laser rockets in *Star Wars*, and the crowd noise in the bar scene of *A Soldier's Story* are all environmental sounds or background sound that help to create the feeling of place and enhance the mood of a piece.

Important Likely Correlations		
Primary Element of Drama ➡	Plot ↓	Character or Thought ↓
Dramatic Action ➡	Physical ↓	Psychological ↓
Major Dramatic Question ➡	What is Going to Happen Next? ↓	What Does This Mean? ↓
Dual Purpose of Arts ➡	Arouse Emotions/Entertain	Stimulate Thought/Instruct

All six of these elements of drama will be used in any theatre arts piece to some degree. Which of the six has the primary and secondary emphasis, will help determine the narrative genre of a piece.

Chapter 3
Genres

The Genre Concept

The genre concept is a method of categorizing a piece. This concept is useful as a basis for thinking about and discussing a piece; a method that gives us a common vocabulary for discussion. *Genres are not mutually exclusive.* In fact, as often as not a piece will be a *mixed genre.* A good example is the common mixture of the genres melodrama and psychological realism. *Fatal Attraction* is a good example. Because character and plot share the emphasis in this film, it is a mixed genre. If one felt that character had more emphasis than plot, then the mixed genre label would be *melodramatic psychological realism.* If, on the other hand, one thought that plot had more emphasis, then the *mixed genre label* would be *psychological melodrama.* The genre with the most emphasis is stated last.

To determine what genre a piece is, the following four areas must be considered:

Determining Genre

1. The relative importance of each of the elements of drama.
2. The nature of the dramatic conflict or dramatic action
3. The degree of verisimilitude.
4. The degree of comedy and/or drama.

The *ordering of the elements of drama* is fundamental to determining the genre of a piece. As one analyzes a piece, one must determine which element of drama, plot, character, thought, diction, spectacle, or music/sound has the primary emphasis. In some cases the emphasis will be shared by two of the elements, which means the piece is a mixed genre.

Generally speaking, one can place the first three elements of drama in the order of emphasis and then the other three together will play a supporting role. It is important to understand that this does not mean that the last two or three elements in a given genre are not important. It simply means they are not dominant. Once the primary element of drama is determined, it is important to analyze how the remainder of the elements relate to and support that primary element.

Dramatic conflict or *dramatic action* is a key to determining which element of drama is emphasized. To create dramatic action, which was discussed in Chapter 2, there must be two opposing forces in conflict. These forces can be as simple as a hero or protagonist in conflict with a villain or antagonist, as in the film *Die Hard*, or as complex as the psychological conflict within a character, as in the film *Rain Man*. The keys to analyzing conflict lie in the following questions.

Analyzing Conflict

1. What is the conflict?
2. What creates the conflict?
3. Is the conflict physical or psychological?
4. What is the basic dramatic question?
5. Out of what element of drama does the conflict primarily arise.

The *degree of verisimilitude*, or how life-like the piece is, can be very important to the genre determination. In one or two genres the order of the elements of drama is basically the same. Therefore, the verisimilitude of the piece can be the determining factor in genre selection.

The same can be said for the *relationship between comedy and drama* in a piece. The reality is that most pieces these days are a combination of comedy and drama. Comedy refers to the emotions of amusement, to things that make us laugh or chuckle or smile happily. Drama refers to the more serious emotions, to things that make us cry or sympathize or empathize and ponder. The term tragedy is not used for serious pieces. We simply do not have tragedy in the classical Aristotelian sense in contemporary theater arts. A society needs a highly structured world view with clearly delineated rules and a sense of universal order to be able to view an event as tragic. Too often what gets labeled as "tragedy" today is simply sentimentalism. The tragic event in these cases is either a matter of bad luck or in some way could have been avoided. A classically tragic event is determined by destiny and is unavoidable. Our contemporary audience is simply not able to view the world in this way. To paraphrase Ionesco, when things become too serious, contemporary society tends to see it as comic. Therefore, serious subjects will often be dealt with in pieces containing a degree of comedy, and these pieces will be labeled drama.

Form is another kind of categorizing that is often confused with the genre concept. *Form is the basic narrative medium in which the material is presented.* The story of Dr.. Jekyll and Mr.. Hyde has been told in many forms, including a novel, a film, a teleplay, a musical, and a play. The genre for all of these forms was "melodrama" or a *mixed genre*—"psychological melodrama"–depending on how much emphasis there was on the psychological make-up of the main character. *Form is a more general kind of categorizing, and any genre can exist in all forms.*

Plot Emphasis Genres

Genres can be divided into two basic groups. Each genre in the first group has plot as primary emphasis. These four genres—melodrama, sentimentalism, situation comedy, and romantic comedy–are all forms of *romanticism*. Each of these genres all present an idealized romantic world where events always end happily–in melodrama good wins over evil, in sentimentalism the family stays together, in situation comedy life's situations are always comic and can be resolved easily, and romantic comedy the right boy always gets the right girl.

Melodrama

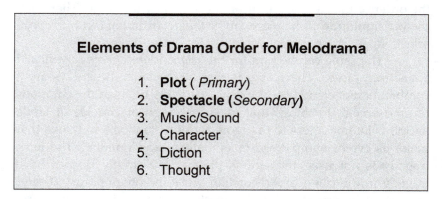

Elements of Drama Order for Melodrama

1. **Plot** (*Primary*)
2. **Spectacle** (*Secondary*)
3. Music/Sound
4. Character
5. Diction
6. Thought

There are two forms of melodrama. Thrillers, science fiction, science fantasy, westerns, adventure films, cops-and-robber movies, and action movies are all labels that are used to describe *action melodrama,* which is probably more popular in film and television than it has ever been. It is popular because it can be some of the best "escapist entertainment" available. In the wonderful tradition of romanticism, good melodrama allows us to believe in heroes and heroines and in the simple concept: good triumphs over evil. *Melodrama has serious physical dramatic action based on a trivial theme.* Melodrama is serious in the sense that the audience fears for the safety of the hero and heroine, but the ideas are too basic or simplistic to be thought provoking. In terms of the "dual purpose of art," melodrama will only set out to entertain us, to arouse our emotions. Romantic melodrama is the second form. Films like *Titanic* and *Varsity Blues* are examples of this form. *Romantic melodrama* emphasizes the romance between the hero and heroine more than action melodrama does, and romantic melodrama does not have the mayhem of action melodrama.

Plot is primary to melodrama. The *basic dramatic question* in melodrama will be "What is going to happen next?" All of the dramatic action, conflict, and interest will be centered around that basic question. In any genre, when "What is going to happen next?" is the primary dramatic question, plot will be very important. The film *Die Hard* is an excellent example of melodrama and the importance of "What is going to happen next?" The plot is a basic linear plot, which is standard in melodrama. All the dramatic action, conflict, and interest stems from the plot and from the audience's concern for the safety of the McClanes as the villains threaten them.

Spectacle will be second in importance, or secondary, in melodrama. Occasionally, spectacle will be so important that it will share the emphasis with plot. A case could be made that the film Star Wars is an example of shared emphasis between plot and spectacle. Generally, however, spectacle will follow plot in emphasis as it does in *Die Hard*. The spectacle in *Die Hard* emphasizes the basic conflict between the hero and the villains. The spectacle is entirely action-oriented as is the conflict. They both are contained in all the fighting, shooting, killing, and explosions that take place throughout this action-oriented melodrama. Here is a gruesome rule about melodrama. Almost without exception, there must be some form of violent death, and this will be part of the spectacle of the piece.

Music and sound will also have some degree of emphasis in the standard melodrama. A background music score is often used to heighten the tension between the hero and the villain. Background sound effects will also be used to accomplish this basic effect. Try to imagine *Die Hard* without all the gunshot noise, fighting noise, and explosions. The film would lose a great deal in terms of dramatic tension if the background music and sound were gone.

Character falls in the lower half of emphasis because of the *degree of development* in melodrama. The characters in melodrama will almost without exception be *one-dimensional*. The characters may seem like they could exist in the "real world," as they do in *Die Hard*, but we will know very little about them psychologically. The hero, McClane, seems real enough but all we really know about him is that he wants his wife and children back in New York with him, and as a cop he represents law and order. He's a "good guy." Hans, the villain, on the other hand, is "evil" incarnate. He not only kills with cold blooded glee but he is a common thief, who is so unprincipled that he claims to be threatening the building and hostages in the name of a political cause in which he has absolutely no belief. But that's it in terms of the traits of these two characters. They are good and evil because more complex characters would interfere with the plot emphasis. We don't need to know more about them psychologically to enjoy the "escapist entertainment" level of the film.

In some cases, the characters in melodrama will be so one-dimensional that they will be caricatures. An obvious example is the film, *Batman*, which was, of course, an adaptation of a comic book. These types of characters are often referred to as "cartoon-like" or "cardboard" in terms of their dimensionality.

Melodrama will usually have a set of "stock" characters. These characters will clearly be good or evil. The good characters will be the hero, heroine, and hero's comic sidekick. The evil characters will consist of the villain, his henchmen, and, at times, a female villain who will tempt the hero toward some sort of evil.

Diction, like all language, must be appropriate and believable in terms of the characters. But in melodrama it will have little emphasis. In Die Hard the diction is primarily used to establish the exposition character traits and will occasionally be used for humor. The diction is typically unexceptional in *Die Hard*.

Thought is of least importance and emphasis in melodrama. The genre simply is not designed to make the audience think at any complex level. Good will always win out over evil in melodrama, which is a highly romantic notion of how life works. This is neither profound nor necessarily very realistic. It is, however, what the audience expects and wants to see. It is a dramatic convention of melodrama.

Sentimentalism

As the Industrial Revolution swept through Europe in the late eighteenth and nineteenth centuries, the emerging middle class wanted a theater that reflected their lives. To meet that need, sentimentalism was born. According to theater historian Oscar Brockett, sentimentalism had "an overemphasis on arousing sympathetic response to the misfortunes of others." This created a style that was called "teary-smiley dialogue." Today's sentimentalism sets out to elicit the same type of response. *Sentimentalism focuses on domestic situations to which an audience can easily identify and with which an audience can sympathize.* An effective sentimental piece will make an audience cry and laugh with tears in their eyes.

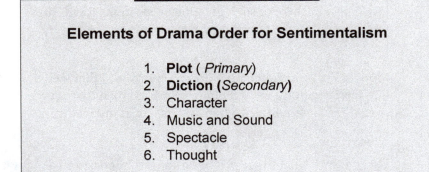

Elements of Drama Order for Sentimentalism

1. **Plot** (*Primary*)
2. **Diction** (*Secondary*)
3. Character
4. Music and Sound
5. Spectacle
6. Thought

As in melodrama, plot will have major emphasis in sentimentalism, and *plot will focus in a serious way on a relatively trivial domestic theme.* The major *plot difference between melodrama and sentimentalism is that the plot in sentimentalism will focus on an element of family life.* Sentimentalism, as melodrama, is also a romantic genre––good will tend to win out over evil, and generally the resolution will be a happy one. The major dramatic question will be "What is going to happen next?"

Television "soap operas" have been the mainstay of this genre in the recent past. It must be pointed out, however, that in current TV soaps, melodrama often creeps in and sometimes dominates. As soon as characters start drawing guns and other characters get shot by those guns, melodrama takes over. This leads to a mixed genre, which is called melodramatic sentimentalism or sentimental melodrama.

In the film, *Terms of Endearment* we find an excellent example of this genre. The *plot* focuses on a mother/daughter relationship and covers a period of about 30 years in that relationship. The main focus is on the mother, Aurora Greenway. She has some trouble showing her love to her daughter, or she does it in an odd way. We learn this in the first scene of the film when her daughter is a baby. Aurora comes rushing into her daughter's room at night to see if she is all right. Aurora tells her husband the baby is not breathing, that maybe she's died of crib death. The husband doubts it. Aurora then pinches the baby, who then starts crying, and Aurora leaves saying, "Oh, she's fine." She is a woman who feels it's necessary to hide her emotions, which is her main character trait. When Aurora's husband dies, she is left to raise her daughter, Emma, and they battle with love through her adolescence. On Emma's wedding night they have the following exchange, which to some degree "foreshadows" Emma's life.

AURORA

I am totally convinced if you marry Flap Norton tomorrow it will be a mistake of such gigantic proportions it will ruin your life and make wretched your destiny.

EMMA

Mother, I'm marrying Flap Norton tomorrow. I thank God for Flap for getting me out of here, and I think if that is your attitude, you shouldn't bother showin' up at my wedding.

AURORA

That's right! No, I think you're right. The hypocrisy was bothering me too.

And she doesn't show up at the wedding. But she does call the newlyweds, and they all make a peace of sorts. Aurora and Flap, however, are polite enemies until the end. All of the conflict grows out of love that clashes with itself. Mother and daughter clash, mother-in-law and son-in-law clash. Husband and wife eventually clash and both have affairs. The young children of Flap and Emma clash with their parents because the children sense the problems in the marriage. Even Aurora's astronaut next-door neighbor, Garrat Breedlove, with whom she finally has an affair and rediscovers love, clash. The conflict is presented in a standard linear plot and developed through the events that happen in the lives of the characters in this family. These events are due more to circumstances in the lives of the characters than out of character development. Thus, the plot is "device driven" and because of these devices the dramatic conflict is considered physical. Much of this conflict is handled in a gently comic way.

We find ourselves sympathizing with the characters and often saying to ourselves, "If only Aurora could show some love, things would get better." Finally she starts to. The beginning of Aurora's change happens when Emma and her family are about to leave Houston to live in Iowa, and the two women are having their goodbye hug.

EMMA

Mama, that's the first time I stopped hugging first. I like that.

AURORA
(looking disturbed)
Get yourself a decent maternity dress.

That's a bittersweet moment in which Aurora still can't face up to her feelings, but at least she's letting them happen.

The major conflict arises when it is discovered that Emma has terminal cancer, a sentimental plot device if there ever was one. How will Aurora and Flap deal with this? What will happen to the three children since Flap is involved with another woman and Emma knows it? Will Garret turn out to be a true jerk or come back to Aurora? All of these questions raised by the plot are concerned with keeping the family together.

The major climax takes place in the hospital room in which Emma is dying and leads to buckets of tears. Suffice it to say the heartstrings are more than adequately tugged and everything resolves itself for the best under the circumstances. Typically, the plot has kept us interested and created the appropriate sympathetic, emotional responses.

Diction is particularly important in sentimentalism because the characters talk more about what they are doing or have done or will do than actually doing it. This is another major difference between melodrama and sentimentalism. In melodrama, characters do a lot and say very little. In sentimentalism the characters say a lot and we see them do very little. In *Terms of Endearment* we not only learn about the characters' thoughts from what they say, but we also learn from their actions. When Garret and Aurora finally get around to spending their first night together in bed, we don't see a fantastic evening of sexual excitement. Instead, we are told about it in a later scene when Emma and Aurora are having a mother and daughter heart to heart talk lying on Aurora's bed. We learn a great deal about the plot and the characters from the diction.

Character is important in sentimentalism because we listen to the characters so much and because the characters *seem like they have a high degree of verisimilitude*. In some examples of this genre, particularly soap operas, the characters will likely be very one-dimensional. Generally speaking, the characters will either be good or evil. However, in the more complex versions of this genre, such as *Terms of Endearment*, the major characters will be somewhat multi-dimensional. In *Terms of Endearment* the complexity of Aurora, Emma, and Garret is limited to how they show love to each other, or, as the title suggests, *their terms of endearment*. Once again, as in all sentimentalism, the issue is *family*. In this case family love, or lack thereof.

Two of the major characters, Aurora and Garret, go through rather major changes. They both, in their own way, learn how to show someone else that they love them. These two brief sections of dialogue indicate the perceived change in Garret. The first takes place when he decides he has become too involved with Aurora.

GARRET

You're some kind of woman. But I'm the wrong kind of man, and it doesn't look like my shot at being the right kind was as good as I was hoping for.

AURORA

You don't even know how much you're going to miss me.

GARRET

I am going to miss you and I feel bad.

AURORA

You're lucky!   I feel humiliated!
(He gets up and walks away.)

After this exchange, we don't see him again until he shows up at the hotel where Aurora is staying in Iowa when Emma is dying. When Aurora sees him, she rushes to him and they embrace and she says, "Who would have expected you to be a nice guy?" and she cries in his arms. It turns out he has changed. Though we're not given much explanation for this, it does make the character more complex and we are happy to see that love has won out.   In *Terms of Endearment* as in most good examples of this genre, the characters have enough verisimilitude to make the audience   easily identify with them. This makes it easier to sympathize with those characters and their situations and thus experience the emotions inherent in the genre.

Music will generally be used to heighten the sympathetic, emotional response. In *Terms of Endearment* music is constantly used to reinforce the sad moments of the piece. It is not used very much other than at those moments; but when the handkerchiefs should come out, the lush, string-filled, symphonic type of music signals it.

Sound and *spectacle* in this genre will be used primarily to help create verisimilitude. *Terms of Endearment* covers roughly a 30 year period from the 1950s through the 1970s, and all the costumes, sets, and environmental sounds help establish an authentic look and sound of each era. *The genre will generally look and sound like the real world.*

Thought will focus on good winning out over evil. The good, in the case of sentimentalism, revolves around the family and its survival and/or improvement. Even though Emma dies, the family unit is perhaps even stronger. It certainly is intact. The three children end up with two parents, Aurora and Garret, who have both found out how to love and presumably will do well raising this new found family. Flap will probably be happier with his graduate student love. Even Emma was happy when she died because she knew her children would be well raised, and she had been loved by her mother and even by her somewhat worthless husband. The family unit survives and all is well with the world. Perhaps not the most realistic outcome, but one that certainly feels good at the end of the film. That too is important in sentimentalism.

Situation Comedy

Elements of Drama Order for Situation Comedy

1. **Plot** (*Primary*)
2. **Spectacle (***Secondary***)**
3. **Diction (***Secondary***)**
4. Character
5. Music and Sound
6. Thought

Situation comedy is as popular a genre as melodrama, and for some of the same reasons. Situation comedy is also purely "escapist entertainment," is also well suited to the camera arts because of the importance of spectacle, and deals with trivial themes, situations that are plot device driven, but purely in a comic sense. All of the elements of drama are designed to make the audience laugh and nothing more. *This genre is built on a plot situation or premise in which characters, whose potential actions or responses are either known by the audience or are predictable, stumble through a comic solution to the premise.* The basic dramatic question in this genre is "What is going to happen next?" Notice how the order of the elements of drama is similar to melodrama.

The *plot* in situation comedy is primary. The exposition will establish the basic premise and the basic character traits for each of the main characters. The dramatic action will be contained within the main characters' attempts to work themselves through the premise. This dramatic action will produce laughter. Television has thrived on situation comedy almost since its inception. Part of the reason for the success of this genre on television lies in the fact that a "sit com" works best in a short time span. Therefore, the half-hour television program is ideal for the genre. In fact, it is much more difficult to write a situation that can sustain itself for the 90-plus minutes needed for a film or a play.

The classic television situation comedy, *The Honeymooners*, is an excellent example of the genre. In the very first episode some of the basic comic "bits" were established so that the audience could begin to predict the nature of the type of situation and the characters' reactions to those situations. In the first scene of that episode, Alice, the wife of the main character, Ralph Kramden (played by one of television's greatest comic actors, Jackie Gleason), rushes into her lower class apartment with a bag of groceries mumbling to herself about being so late. Almost immediately, her neighbor and best friend Trixie, comes through the door and says,

> TRIXIE
>
> What's for dinner?

> ALICE
> (taking things out of shopping bag)
> Frozen peas, carrots, french fries, steak, bowling ball.

> TRIXIE
>
> Bowling ball? Isn't that a little heavy for dinner?

> ALICE
>
> Huh? Oh, that's Ralph's new bowling ball. That's why I'm
> so late for dinner. I had to go all the way downtown
> to a sporting goods store to get it for him.

> TRIXIE
>
> You'd better get Ralph's dinner on the table. I've got Ed's
> feast all set. You know that bowling tournament starts in an
> hour.

> ALICE
>
> I had no idea it was so late!

In this very brief exchange, the situation and basic relationships are established. Almost immediately following this exchange, Ralph and Ed Norton, Trixie's husband, come home from work. Ralph sees the bowling ball and is very happy with it. Trixie and Norton leave. Ralph asks about his dinner and the episode is off into the complications. The dinner can't be made until it thaws, which will make Ralph late for his bowling tournament. He decides to open a can of beans. He needs to get a hammer to get the can opener into the top of the bean can because Alice has dulled the point using the can opener for a screw driver. He whacks his thumb with the hammer and proceeds to get it stuck in the bowling ball. Norton shows up to go bowling and helps Ralph get the bowling ball off his thumb. Ralph decides he can't go because his thumb is swollen. Norton leaves. Ralph rants and raves. Alice has really done it this time, and Ralph utters the classic line, "One of these days, Alice! One of these days! Pow! Right in the kisser." In later episodes this line becomes a signature line for the series, "One of these days, to the moon Alice!" Both of these lines are accompanied by a round house upper-cut swing of the arm and fist. At which point Alice points out that it's his left thumb that is hurt and he bowls with his right hand. Ralph heads toward the door to leave and Alice wishes him good luck. Ralph turns back, apologizes, wonders how she can live with him, and invites her to come along to watch, which she does.

The nature of the comedy in this drama will determine the order of these three elements of drama, *spectacle, diction,* and *character.* If the humor is generated out of the *physical activity of the characters,* like the can opener and bowling bowl described above, then spectacle would fall into the secondary emphasis position. This type of humor is called "farcical humor."

Farcical humor comes in the stock form of pies in the face, pratfalls, mistaken identity, and other physical action. In *The Honeymooners* episode Ralph exaggerated his reaction both to hitting his thumb and getting his thumb stuck in the bowling ball by howling and stomping around the room like a wounded elephant. This overreaction is in counterpoint to Alice, who sits calmly in her chair waiting for him to finish his tirade. As the series goes on this becomes a stock reaction on the part of both characters. Ralph rants and Alice patiently waits for him to finish and then she solves the problem. This physical activity of Ralph's is farcical, and rarely fails to be humorous. Of course, you have to see it to find the humor. But that's the point of this type of humor.

If the *humor comes from what the characters say,* the *diction* then becomes secondary. If there is little or no farcical humor then spectacle will fall into the lower half of the order of the elements of drama. In *The Honeymooners* there is a fair amount of *language humor* or *line humor.* An example is the following.

ALICE
I can't cook the food until it thaws out.

RALPH
What are we having, snowballs?

Following this are a half dozen more cold-food jokes of this nature. In *The Honeymooners* the farcical humor and the diction or language or line humor are about equal. For that reason, spectacle and diction have shared importance as secondary elements of drama. This is fairly common in situation comedy.

Character in situation comedy will be psychologically one-dimensional, as it is in melodrama. The audience must be able to predict the behavior of the characters in order to find them funny. That does not mean that the audience has to know exactly what a character is going to say or do, but we must have a general idea so we can anticipate Ralph's reaction to something Alice has done.

Music and *sound* will be used to reinforce the humor. The music will generally be light and lively to help establish the mood. Occasionally musical themes will be developed for certain characters or certain types of situations to help the audience know these characters are coming or situations are about to happen. The sound effects will have whatever degree of verisimilitude is necessary to make the characters and situations believable within the world created by the piece. Often the sound effects will be heightened or exaggerated for comic effect.

Thought will be of little or no importance. Situation comedy does not attempt to make an audience think or instruct its members in any way. The purpose of situation comedy is to arouse the emotions of joy, to make us smile, chuckle, giggle, and belly laugh. When it is inventive and original, it can be another wonderful escapist entertainment genre.

Romantic Comedy

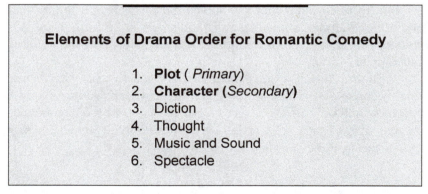

Elements of Drama Order for Romantic Comedy

1. **Plot** (*Primary*)
2. **Character (***Secondary***)**
3. Diction
4. Thought
5. Music and Sound
6. Spectacle

The key to romantic comedy is centered in a romantic or idealized outlook on life in general and love in particular. In the romantic world-view everything in life comes out as it would in an ideal world. Romantic comedy, as well as melodrama and sentimentalism, are direct descendants of *romanticism*, which flourished during the 1800s in European drama and literature. *A romantic comedy will present outcomes in love relationships, as they would be in a perfect world.* The notion of "viewing life through rose colored glasses" is at the heart of romantic comedy. The films *Four Weddings and a Funeral*, *You've Got Mail* and *Moonstruck* are all excellent examples of romantic comedy.

In romantic comedy, *character* and *plot* will often have equal emphasis. Though the characters in contemporary romantic comedy will seem to have a great deal of verisimilitude, the romantic nature of the plot will determine the final outcome of a piece. *As often as not, the basic plot structure will be the standard boy meets girl, boy loses girl, boy gets girl.* In the film *Moonstruck* the two main characters create the conflict through their relationship.

The female lead, Loretta, is a very sensible woman with a good job but has been "unlucky in love." In her mid-thirties, she has decided to marry a man she likes, who needs her, but whom she doesn't love. She lives at home with her tightly knit Italian family, and they are to various degrees pleased with this arrangement. All of these characters are played with a great deal of verisimilitude, with a degree of Italian family stereotyping–but they are believable characterizations, not caricature. The characters, especially Loretta, are multidimensional.

In the exposition it is revealed that Loretta's husband to be, Johnny, must go to Italy before their marriage to be with his dying mother. They will marry when he gets back, and Loretta will make all the arrangements. As Johnny leaves for Italy, he asks Loretta to invite his brother, Ronnie, to the wedding. Loretta does not know Ronnie but sets out to find him and extend the invitation to him.

In romantic comedy there will often be one character that is the "romantic character." This character will tend to be the most emotional, have the most idealized romantic view of life. This character will also have the least degree of verisimilitude. In contemporary romantic comedy, this character's romanticism will usually be justified somehow either through a plot device and/or through some psychological trauma. In *Moonstruck*, Ronnie is that principal romantic character. Loretta goes to see Ronnie and finds him in the basement of his bakery where he is baking bread with coal-fired ovens. While surrounded by his understanding employees, he and Loretta have the following exchange:

RONNIE

I have no life. My brother, Johnny, took my life from me....
(addressing a female employee)
Get me the big knife. I'm going to cut my throat.
(to Loretta)
You can watch and tell Johnny about it on his wedding day....Do you know about me?

LORETTA

No.

RONNIE

O.K. Nothing is anybody's fault, but things happen. Look....

> (he holds up his left hand and slowly
> pulls off a glove revealing a wooden
> hand)

This wood, this fake. Five years ago I was engaged to be married and Johnny came in here and he ordered bread from me. I said, O.K., some bread, and I put my hand in the slicer. It got caught because I wasn't paying attention. The slicer chewed off my hand. It's funny because when my fianceé found out about it, found out I had been maimed, she left me for another man.

LORETTA

So that's the bad blood between you and Johnny?

RONNIE

Yes. That's it.

LORETTA

That's not Johnny's fault!

RONNIE

> (knocking a large can of flour off
> a table and screams at her)

I don't care! I ain't no freakin' monument to justice! I lost my hand! I lost my bride! Johnny has his hand! Johnny has his bride! You want me to take my heartbreak, put it away and forget it.

As he walks away into another room, the female employee says with tears in her eyes, "This is the most tormented man I have ever known. I love this man, but I've never told him because he could never love anybody since he lost his hand and his girl."

Clearly Ronnie's "torment" lacks a degree of verisimilitude, but as a romantic character he is believable. In terms of the plot structure, the boy and the girl have met.

Loretta asks Ronnie if they can talk privately somewhere, and they go to his apartment above the bakery. Her desire to help gets the best of her, they talk, she makes him lunch, they argue a bit about who has been the biggest fool in love, and then they impulsively make love–*boy gets girl*. The next morning, Loretta feels very guilty and says.

LORETTA

I'm going to marry him–Johnny! Do you hear me. Last
night never happened and I'm going to marry him and you
are going to take this to your coffin.

RONNIE

I can't do that.

LORETTA

Why not?

RONNIE

I'm in love with you.

LORETTA
(Loretta slaps Johnny on the face)
Snap out of it.

She leaves promising to see him one more time at the opera
that night, but then it will be over–*boy loses girl*.

The conflict in the remainder of the film has to do with this
love triangle and *boy getting girl back*. Thus, the major dramatic
question is, "What will happen next?" This conflict is both plot and
character driven. The comedy also arises both from the plot and the
characters. There is a shared emphasis between character and plot.

Diction is important because the characters have a fair degree
of verisimilitude and usually talk a great deal about their romantic
point of view. Also, most of the humor is language based, not
physical.

Thought is usually fairly simplistic and has a strong romantic
emphasis. For some, that means the thought is not very much like the
real world. Remember the romantic world is an idealized world. So
the thought in romantic comedy will have everyone and everything
ending up happy.

In *Moonstruck*, there is a significant subplot involving Loretta's
father, Cosmos, and an affair he is having, as well as a potential affair
Loretta's mother could have but doesn't. All of the conflict is finally
resolved in the last scene, which takes place in the family kitchen
at breakfast around the kitchen table. Johnny and Ronnie resolve
their conflict, Mother and Father resolve their conflict, and Loretta
and Ronnie will be married and live happily ever after. The main
thought seems to be that family love and romantic love can conquer
all. A lovely romantic thought, though perhaps not profound, nor

realistic. This is generally the depth of thought in romantic comedy.

Symbolism often plays a key role in this genre. The title in *Moonstruck* is a good example. The night that Ronnie and Loretta end up in bed there is a huge moon, which all of the characters observe and are romantically influenced by, they're "moonstruck." It's a very obvious symbol but nonetheless a symbol.

Another obvious symbol is the wooden hand that Ronnie has. This symbolizes both the romantic nature of the character and his "torment." At one point Loretta refers to Ronnie as a wolf caught in a trap. The trap was the girl he was in love with. Like a wolf, in order to get out of that trap he allowed his hand to be chewed off. This is typical of the type of symbolism one finds in the genre.

Music is used to establish and enhance the mood in romantic comedy. In *Moonstruck* the music is used to establish the ethnic nature of the characters as well as the mood. The music includes Italian operatic arias as well as 1950s type songs such as Dean Martin's version of *Volare*. The music itself was romantic in style and thus enhanced the film genre.

The *sound* used in Moonstruck has a high degree of verisimilitude, which is typical for the genre. But it also is used to emphasize mood in some cases. A good example of this takes place in a dinner table scene. Loretta's mother, father, grandfather, aunt, and uncle are having dinner. Loretta's place is set, but she is at that moment in bed with Ronnie. None of the other characters knows this, of course. Also, Loretta's father has previously spent the afternoon with his girlfriend and feels guilty about it. There is tension in the room, but no one knows why or admits it. This tension is heightened by the exaggerated sounds of knives and forks on plates and people chewing and drinking. The sounds have a high degree of verisimilitude, but the mood is enhanced by the increased emphasis on the sounds.

Spectacle will have a degree of verisimilitude in the genre but will often be selective. In Moonstruck all of the sets seem to be "location" sets, the real thing: an actual apartment, restaurant, bakery, etc. But it all has a certain gloss to it. The photography and the lighting are very pretty, very romantic looking. This too is typical of the genre.

In romantic comedy, while there will be a high degree of verisimilitude, all of the elements of drama will be contributing to the basic idealized view of a romantic world. The events and characters portrayed will be treated humorously and all will come out happy in the end.

Character /Thought Genres

The second basic group of genres has character and/or thought as primary emphasis. These three genres–psychological realism, abstract realism and dark comedy–deal with issues in a way that is usually more like real life and thus more often than not these genres do not end happily. All three of these genres will accomplish both of the dual purposes of art. They will arouse emotions and stimulate thought.

Psychological Realism

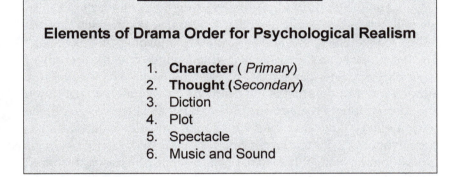

Elements of Drama Order for Psychological Realism

1. **Character** (*Primary*)
2. **Thought (***Secondary***)**
3. Diction
4. Plot
5. Spectacle
6. Music and Sound

Playwright Henrik Ibsen is often called "the father of modern drama." With the production of Ibsen's *A Doll's House* in 1879, psychological realism was born. Following its success, the genre dominated the theater for the next 100 years. While no longer dominate in today's theater, psychological realism remains a major genre in film and television. The reason for this shift lies in the basic elements of the genre. *Psychological realism deals with the psychological make-up of the characters presented by the piece as they would exist in the "real world."* The camera arts can obviously portray "real world characters" in a "real world" more effectively than can theater.

In psychological realism, *character* has the major emphasis, it is primary. Generally there will only be a few characters portrayed and these characters will be *multi-dimensional*. The academy award winning film, *Rain Man*, is an excellent example of psychological realism. In this film, there are two major characters and one supporting character who are extensively developed in terms of their psychological character traits. The protagonist, main character, is Charlie Babbit. By the end of the film the audience knows the most about him and has seen him go through a significant psychological change.

In the beginning of the film, Charlie is set up as a good looking, likable scoundrel. He's working a deal to sell four very expensive cars at a huge profit but has run into a problem clearing them through EPA emissions requirements. In spite of this, he and Suzanna, his girlfriend and partner, are off to a vacation in Palm Springs. On the way, a call on his car phone informs him his father has died. We discover that he and his father have not spoken for years because "nothing I did was good enough for this guy." Charlie explains this to Suzanna in defense of his separation from his father.

By the time the funeral is over, we know that Charlie is cold and distant because his cold and distant father raised him after his mother died when he was two. All of this information is exposition to set up who Charlie is and how he thinks and feels as well as to set up the basic situation.

The *inciting incident* is the reading of the father's will. In his will, the father leaves Charlie a 1949 Buick Roadmaster and the father's prize roses, "so he can know the meaning of excellence." The rest of the $3 million estate is left to a blind trust, the identity of which is to remain a secret from Charlie. Charlie quickly discovers the administrator of the trust is the head of a private mental institution and then accidentally discovers his unknown brother, Raymond, the second main character, a "high functioning autistic savant" who has been living at the institution since Charlie was two. Charlie kidnaps him so that he can get his share of the $3 million. It is at this point that the supporting character, Suzanna, leaves him saying,

SUZANNA
They tell you, 'you have a brother', and I don't see one reaction. You tell me lies.

CHARLIE
What is my crime?

SUZANNA
You use people, you use me, you use Raymond, you use everybody!

CHARLIE
Raymond am I using you, am I using you Raymond!

RAYMOND
Yes.

CHARLIE
Shut up! He's answering a question from a half hour ago.

We have learned about Charlie through what he says and does and through what others have said about him.

The film at this point has established a *high degree of verisimilitude* along with a mood that is serious but with a touch of humor, as the previous exchange suggests. Raymond's response, "yes," is comical because it is so unexpected and so true. Until this point, all that Raymond has done and said seemed without logic. In fact, we are told by a minor character, who is a male nurse in the institution in which Raymond lives, that Raymond is bound by routines and that any break in a routine terrifies him. When that happens he starts to recite the Abbott and Costello routine, "Who's On First?," which he does rather often throughout the film. More often than not, this also produces a comic effect for the audience that is tinged with sympathetic understanding. All of what we have seen in this film to this point, and all that will follow as the two brothers travel across the country and Charlie gets to know a lost brother, as well as new things about himself, is developed through the "real world" psychological make-up of the characters in the film. Importantly, these are characters with whom we can identify and believe in the "real world."

The *conflict* in this film is primarily psychological conflict of character. There is a minor plot conflict in terms of Charlie's efforts to get his half of the $3 million. Because of this plot conflict the dramatic question "What is going to happen next?" does arise. But it is not the predominant dramatic question in psychological realism. Importantly, this basic linear plot is created because of Charlie's own character traits and those of his dead father. The main conflict has to do with Charlie's ability to cope with Raymond, to handle the responsibility of caring for Raymond, and finally his ability to deal with the psychological conflict within himself as he learns to love another person. All of this is tied into the psychological make-up of Charlie.

Thus, in this film, as in all psychological realism, the basic dramatic question is "What does this mean?" and the element of drama, *thought*, has strong secondary emphasis. The *meaning* or *thought* in a piece will generally be tied into the *change that takes place in the protagonist*. But the ideas of a piece are not necessarily limited to the protagonist's change. This change often takes place during the final climax of a piece, at which point the protagonist makes a "discovery" and then "reverses" his previous action. In Aristotelian terms this is called "discovery and reversal." In *Rain Man* there is a specific example of this principle.

The major climax comes in the office of the psychiatrist who is to give the court his opinion about who should have custody of

Raymond. While the psychiatrist is questioning Raymond to a point of almost frantic confusion, Charlie insists that they stop. It is at this point that he "discovers" that he cannot take care of Raymond, and though he has come to love him, he must let him go back to the institution in Ohio. He has "reversed" his goals. He has changed greatly from the beginning of the film. No longer does he only look out and care for his own well-being, but the well-being of someone he loves has become more important to him than his own. This change has been made believable through the psychological make-up of the three principal characters in the film. The main thought in *Rain Man* is tied into this change in Charlie and to a lesser degree in a slight change in Raymond, who in theory could not change at all because of the nature of his mental condition. The idea can be stated simply as "caring for another person can make you a different person." That's probably too simplistic for this complex film, but that can happen when you're trying to simplify.

In psychological realism the thought and the characters are tied together in a way that makes them both believable in the "real world."

In the scene following Charlie's discovery and reversal, Charlie and Raymond are alone in the psychiatrist's office. They are seated next to each other. Charlie has his hand around Raymond's shoulder and they are very close together. Normally Raymond would move away from this kind of closeness but he doesn't at this point.

CHARLIE
I just want you to know that what I said about being on the road with you. I meant, connecting. I like having you for my brother.

RAYMOND
I'm an excellent driver.

CHARLIE
Yes you are.
(Raymond leans his head against Charlie's as the camera zooms s lowly in)

RAYMOND
I like having you for my big brother.
(Charlie rises slowly and kisses Raymond on the forehead)
C-h-a-r-l-i-e main man.

From the actions and the dialogue of this scene we understand the feelings of the characters. The character relationships and dramatic action have *aroused our emotions* in many ways. We understand the connection these two characters have made and can *think about these ideas in terms of our own lives and world.* The piece has accomplished the dual purpose of art.

The *diction* in psychological realism will sound like it belongs in the "real world." It is essential that what we hear the characters say in this genre has strong verisimilitude to the type of "real world" characters they represent. The nature of the language in *Rain Man* is very "real world" believable. Even though most of us would not have any experience with an autistic savant like Raymond, the dialogue seemed totally appropriate. It was reported in several articles about this film that Dustin Hoffman, who played the character Raymond, spent a considerable amount of time with an autistic savant in order to accurately portray the proper physical and vocal mannerisms. We can thus assume from that knowledge that the dialogue was "real." More importantly for the audience, the rhythms, sentence structure, and word choices for this character, as for all the characters in the film, sounded believable in the "real world." That is key to believable diction or language in this genre.

The *plot* in this genre will more often than not be *linear*. Since most of us experience the real world in a chronologically linear way, psychological realism works best when the plot follows that "real world" formula. *Rain Man* is linear from beginning to end. It does, in fact, fit rather neatly into the basic linear structure outlined in Chapter 2. However, in this genre, the plot will develop because of the psychological make-up of the characters. In *Rain Man* the reason that Charlie and Raymond must spend so much time together is that Raymond is terrified of flying. The first time we see Raymond go into a fit of uncontrollable fright is when Charlie tries to force him on a plane. This plot change comes out of a deep psychological fear within the character, not out of a manipulated plot device, as would so often be the case in a plot-oriented genre like melodrama. Thus, in psychological realism the *plot is character driven*.

The *spectacle* in psychological realism will also have a *high degree of verisimilitude*. The places will look like the real places they represent. The actors will look and dress like the characters they are playing would look in the real world. There will be little emphasis on spectacle except that it must look "real world." For that reason, Rain Man scenes that take place in a warehouse were shot in a warehouse. Scenes that took place in Las Vegas in a casino were shot in Las Vegas in a casino. If a scene wasn't shot "on location," the studio set was made to look as much like the "real" location as possible. In psychological realism, the spectacle must look like the "real world" so that we can believe the psychological make-up of the characters. This idea is not just true for the camera arts but also for theater. For this reason, we see less and less psychological realism in theater. The camera arts can simply create the spectacle of the real world more easily and convincingly.

The *music* for this genre will be used to establish the relative seriousness of a given piece. Since there can be a mixture of comedy and drama in psychological realism, the music can help tell the audience what the combination of comedy and drama will be and when things will be comic and when dramatic. In *Rain Man* there was one particular segment that best exemplifies this point. Charlie and Raymond are in the bathroom of a motel room with Raymond brushing his teeth. Charlie turns on the hot water in the bathtub and Raymond becomes terrified

RAYMOND
(screaming)
Hot water burn baby!

CHARLIE
That's why they put you away. They thought you would hurt me.

RAYMOND
(whispering)
Never would hurt Charlie Babbit.

At this point very quiet, gentle, tender music "plays under" the dialogue as Raymond repeats his last line over several times. The mood is reinforced by the music. This cuts to the next day, the sun is shining, and they are traveling down the road with the top down in the Buick convertible. Raymond is smiling. Charlie is happier. They are moving on, both down the road and in their relationship. The music is very up, disco like, high energy to match the new mood of the new scene.

The *sound* for psychological realism will, on the other hand, be used to reinforce the verisimilitude. The sound effects will relate directly to what we see on-screen or to what is referred to off-screen: a door shutting, a dog barking, or bathwater running into a bathtub as it did in the scene described above. The sound effects in that scene were loud and helped create a sense of excitement and concern for the audience when Raymond became terrified by the memory of the baby being burned in the bathwater.

When the music took over to change the mood of the moment the sound effects completely disappeared. Because we are so accustomed to background music in film, it has become a dramatic convention and we accept it as believable, even though we know in the "real world" situation this film was portraying music won't suddenly take over and replace the "real" sounds of the environment. The filmmaker established in the very first scene of the film that background music would be used to create mood, in spite of the verisimilitude of the other elements in the film. Had he not done this, music in the middle of such a dramatic scene as was just described would not have worked. A film with an almost "naturalistic" verisimilitude like the film, *Drugstore Cowboy*, would not use music in the way *Rain Man* did but instead relies more on sound effects to help establish mood and verisimilitude. Even though music and sound have the least emphasis in the genre, they are still of a high degree of importance. Music and sound, like the other supportive elements in this genre, reinforce character, the primary element of drama in psychological realism.

Abstract Realism

Elements of Drama Order for Abstract Realism

1. **Thought** (*Primary*)
2. **Character** (*Secondary*)
3. **Spectacle** (*Secondary*)
4. Diction
5. Music and Sound
6. Plot

Even though psychological realism dominated the theater for almost a century, there has been a continuing number of theater artists working in other less realistic styles. Some of these styles include the "relativist theater" of Luigi Pirandello, the "existentialist theater" of Jean Paul Sartre and Albert Camus, and various artists working in expressionism, dadaism, surrealism, and futurism. The most important of these styles are the "epic theater" of Bertolt Brecht and the "absurdist theater" of Eugene Ionesco, Samuel Beckett, and others. All of these various nonrealistic styles emphasized the importance of the uniqueness of the theater as a medium. They came under a general category that has been called "theatricalism" or "non-realistic theater." Both of these terms are somewhat misleading, at least in terms of today's contemporary theater. Producer Richard Barr coined the term that better describes the genre of the majority of contemporary plays in the early 1970s. That term is *abstract realism*.

Abstract realism owes its heritage to the realistic approach of Ibsen, to the existentialism of Sartre and Camus, to the theatricality of the absurdists, and most importantly to German playwright and theorist Bertolt Brecht. *Brecht wanted a theater that forced the audience to think.* He felt that psychological realism allowed the audience to lose itself in the emotions of the characters and that when the audience became too much involved with feeling they stopped thinking. Brecht wanted to instruct the audience as well as entertain them. In order to do this, he developed what are called "alienation devices". These are manipulations in a play that remind the audience they are seeing a play. They are in a theater. Therefore, Brecht's plays were staged so that the stage itself was apparent. Theater lights, the backstage area, actors changing costumes or watching other actors as they performed were common. Sets were simplified and "suggestive." Two wooden boxes and a plank would become a bridge and later would be a bench in a courtroom scene. The audience was asked to use its imagination more, to think more, and to remember they were in a theater watching a play that meant something to them. But the "alienation devices" weren't just physical, as can be seen in his play *The Caucasian Chalk Circle*. Brecht stops a plot line just at the point he felt an audience would be getting too involved with the plot or the characters. He moves to a new situation and later ties the two seemingly unrelated plots together to make his point. In another point in the play, Brecht has a character do something totally out of character or illogical. All of this was designed to keep the audience thinking about the ideas of the play, which in Brecht's case was Marxist philosophy.

The "absurdists" that followed Brecht, most notably in France, Ionesco and Beckett, took Brecht's concepts a bit further and intellectually in another direction. Speaking of the absurdists, critic Martin Esslin in his book, "The Theater of the Absurd", writes: the theater must work with veritable shock tactics; reality itself, the consciousness of the spectator, his habitual apparatus of thought-language-must be overthrown, dislocated, turned inside out, so that he suddenly comes face to face with a new perception of reality.[1]

Philosophically the absurdists advocated an existentialist view of life. Their basic premise was that if one doesn't take responsibility for one's own existence, it can become absurd. Their plays tended to show the audience this absurdity. They took an abstract concept and made it concrete. Critic Esslin explains that the absurdists had a tendency "to express psychological states by objectifying them on stage."[2] This process is called "objectifying the subjective." *Abstract realism takes basically realistic characters and/or situations and in some way abstracts them.* The abstraction can come in almost any form and be presented through any or all elements of drama. The reason for doing this is to make the audience think about the ideas of the piece. Therefore, the dramatic question, "What does this mean?" will be dominant in abstract realism.

Thought will have the emphasis in this genre. Oftentimes the thought will focus on a comment about society or have a strong philosophical point of view. Director Terry Gilliam's film, *Brazil*, is a good example of this. In the film, Gilliam is making a comment about the potential danger of an overly centralized form of government. In order to make it clear that he is not talking about a specific form of government, he starts off by telling us that the film takes place "somewhere in the twentieth century." He creates a world that is different from any we know but has elements that are recognizable in our world. Much of the comment in the film concerning the rigidly structured nature of the society is presented through comic satire. Satire is often a key to the humor in abstract realism.

As is often the case in psychological realism, the basic philosophical thought in *Brazil* has to do with the narrow line between *illusion and reality*. The main character, Sam Lowery, is introduced to the audience for the first time in a dream in which he has great beautiful silver wings and is flying through billowy white clouds. We don't realize this is a dream until a jarring buzzing disturbs the flying sequence, and the film cuts to Sam grabbing his telephone as he has been jolted out of his sleep. As the film moves along, Sam's dreams and his "real" life become more and more the same until the final scene when he has, as one character says, "slipped away from us" into his dream world, which is then his new reality. Director Gilliam has objectified Sam's subjective dream world by showing it to us and in the final scene of the film, making us think that the illusion is reality.

The *dramatic conflict* in abstract realism will be primarily *psychological*. In this film the psychological conflict has to do with the individual's will and struggle against a controlling, paternalistic society. This concept is the *social thought or message of the film*. Sam is content in this society until he sees a girl who is being investigated by the Department of Information Retrieval. This girl is literally the girl of his dreams. She appears in his dreams in a cage, and he tries to rescue her. It turns out she may be a terrorist and she is being investigated. As in his dream, in his "real" world he tries to rescue her. To further tie the reality/illusion theme and the social comment together, the question is raised as to whether or not there are actually terrorists. Or has the government created terrorists to have an enemy for the citizens to be worried about? Are the terrorists an illusion? Certainly Sam and his girlfriend are not terrorists. But in the end they are dealt with as though they are. The final scene leaves us with a chilling resolution. The government has maintained total control through force. Sam, to escape torture, has disappeared into his world of illusion. As an audience, we are left with countless ideas to ponder and to ask ourselves: How does the world of this piece relate to my world? How does Sam's struggle with illusion and reality relate to me or people I know? "What does this mean?"

The main *characters* in abstract realism will often be multi-dimensional. Though many times this will simply be a single main character and the remainder of the characters will be one-dimensional. This is clearly the case in *Brazil*. We see a relatively complex character in Sam as he moves about in his world, both dream and real. We come to an understanding of the psychological complexity of Sam. The other characters in the film are very one-dimensional, however. They are basically believable, even in our world. But, they are primarily one-dimensional. Even though we see a lot of the girl, all we really know about her is that she is a beautiful truck driver who is concerned about other people. This pattern is typical of the genre. One or two characters will be multi-dimensional and the remainder will be one-dimensional.

Spectacle will often share the secondary emphasis with character in abstract realism. *Many times the abstraction will take place in the spectacle.* This is certainly the case in *Brazil*. The sets and costumes create a world like one we have not known, but it has a sense of the real world in it. This is done primarily through exaggeration and incongruity. The government buildings are too massive, too stark. Though there are computers, they have keyboards like the typewriters of the 1940s. The designers of this film have done a wonderful job of creating a world that reflects, that symbolizes, the massive control of the central government. We see this control long before we're told about it. We see the ideas through the spectacle as well as hear it through the dialogue.

Diction in this genre will, for the most part, seem primarily like the real world. This will be particularly true for the main character because that character will be the most complex psychologically. The protagonist will often have the majority of the dialogue. This is certainly true of Sam in *Brazil*. The diction for the supporting and minor characters will often be very specifically tailored to the one-dimensionality of those characters. Sam's supervisor at Information Retrieval is a good example of this. Every word he utters suggests a low level administrator who wants nothing to go wrong in his department because he is terrified of being noticed by upper-level administrators. The following exchange between Sam and his boss, Mr.. Kurtzman, takes place when Kurtzman discovers a potential mistake with which he does not know how to deal.

Sam comes through the door of Kurtzman's office after

being summoned by Kurtzman. Upon entering the   office, Sam looks around for him. Kurtzman seems not to be in the office, then emerges cautiously from behind a filing cabinet and tiptoes to the door making certain no one sees him and quietly shuts the door.

                    KURTZMAN
Thank God your here. We're in terrible trouble. Look at this! Look at this!

                    SAM
It's a check.

                    KURTZMAN
It's the refund for Tuttle.

                    SAM
Tuttle?

                    KURTZMAN
Buttle! I mean Buttle! It's confusion from the word go. He's been charged for information retrieval procedure. And someone, somewhere is trying to make us carry the blame.

                    SAM
Can I have a look. I've never seen a refund check before.

                    KURTZMAN
I'll bet it's Jeffries. He always believes people should pay more for their interrogation and he loathes me. How can we get rid of it?

It turns out Buttle is dead. They then try to deposit the check in   Buttle's wife's bank account, but that doesn't work because she has no bank account. Kurtzman is sure they are doomed.

                    KURTZMAN
Well that's it then. I might just as well hang myself now. This sort of thing could never have happened before that stupid seventh tier reorganization. That's Simmon's doing. And he and Jeffries always sit together at lunch. Bastards!

He personifies the fear of the control by the central government. *The diction in this film not only helps us understand the psychological make-up of the main character and his world of illusion and reality but also reinforces the main social theme concerning the negative effect of the controlling central government.*

Music and Sound can be used either to reinforce the psychological verisimilitude of the characters or as an element of the abstraction. In *Brazil* music is used to reinforce the abstraction. In fact, the title of the film comes from the song *Brazil*, which was a popular song of the 1940s and had a Latin beat. The words and melody are used throughout the film. The melody is treated in every way from ethereal to terrorizing. The original popular version opens and closes the film. At the end of the film, Sam is sitting in a chair that looks quite like an electric chair in the middle of the interrogation room, which seems like the inside of a deserted nuclear power plant, and the final lyrics of *Brazil* are played.

> *Tomorrow was another day*
> *The morning found me miles away*
> *With still a million things to say.*
> *Now,*
> *as twilight beams from the sky above*
> *recalling the thrill of our love*
> *there's one thing I'm certain of*
> *return*
> *I will to old*
> *Brazil.*

As the lyric ends, Sam is seated in his chair in the middle of those billowy clouds of his dreams. The song has symbolized a world of his illusions, and he has now entered it permanently. *The music has helped objectify the subjective.*

The *sound*, on the other hand, helps to create the environment in Brazil. The mechanized world created in Brazil is reinforced by the sounds we hear. This is particularly true when we see the odd computers in this world and when the huge heating and cooling duct work, which is everywhere, breaks down or is blown up. *In this film the sound helps to create the world of the piece and make it believable.*

Plot in abstract realism will usually have the least emphasis and will tend to be *episodic*, though linear plots can exist in this genre. Though there is a fair amount of plot in *Brazil*, it is a good example of how a plot can jump around from place to seemingly unrelated place and in and out of reality and illusion. In the first five minutes the audience is taken from Sam's dream world, to the Buttle's' apartment, to Jill's bathtub, to Kurtzman's office, back to Sam's dream world, with Jill in a cage, and finally to Sam's bedroom. There is no apparent connection to any of these places or what takes place in them in these first five minutes. It takes most of the remainder of the film to piece it all together. The episodic nature of the plot keeps the audience asking, "What does this mean?" In this way the plot helps the audience to focus on the major element of drama in the genre, thought.

Dark Comedy

The most serious comic genre is dark comedy because it usually has a serious, thought- provoking ending and very often focuses on social issues from a satirical point of view. An audience will generally laugh at the humor until they realize the serious nature of the ideas being explored by dark comedy. This genre accomplishes the dual purpose of art by making the audience laugh at the characters and/ or situations portrayed and then making the audience think, "But, what does this mean?"

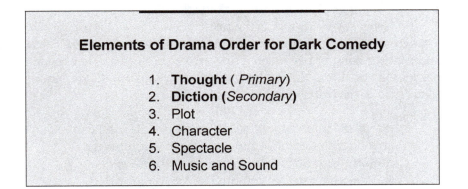

Elements of Drama Order for Dark Comedy

1. **Thought** (*Primary*)
2. **Diction (***Secondary***)**
3. Plot
4. Character
5. Spectacle
6. Music and Sound

Like abstract realism, in dark comedy *thought* is emphasized. Dark comedy, however, tends to focus on social issues more than psychological issues. Also, dark comedy always emphasizes the comic aspects of plot and character. Whereas, abstract realism is either comic or serious depending on the piece. The other major distinction between the two genres is that dark comedy does not have any abstraction and thus seems to have more verisimilitude than abstract realism. Though thought is central to both genres, the approach to the thought is rather significantly different.

Stanley Kubrick's hilarious film, *Dr. Strangelove or: How I Learned To Stop Worrying and Love the Bomb,* is a wonderful example of dark comedy. The main thought has to do with the futility of the nuclear arms race. This idea is presented in this film primarily through satire. The basic notion of competitive buildup of nuclear arms between two superpowers as a means of deterrence is taken to an absurd but plausible conclusion–the world is destroyed because of a military madman and a "doomsday device" that is so horrible a weapon it is supposed to prevent nuclear attack. The audience is left to question, "Could this kind of nuclear madness take place under the present circumstances? How far off is this fictional, satirical, dark comedy from the real world of nuclear buildup, anti-nuclear satellites, and Stealth Bombers that we live in?" Thought is the focus in this typical example of the genre, and we see these ideas reflected and reinforced by the other elements of drama.

The dramatic conflict in this genre is partially created by the opposing forces within the major thought presented by the piece. These opposing ideas are primarily presented through diction. The comedy will be generally word oriented with a focus on *wit, irony, and exaggeration,* which are the *chief devices of satire.* *Dr. Strangelove* while incorporating a degree of physical comedy, basically relies on exposing the foolishness of the military and political leaders who advocate nuclear deterrence as an avenue to peace. This is done primarily through the dialogue of the piece, in which the military takes the brunt of Kubrick`s satirical attack.

General Jack Ripper is the principal military madman in *Dr. Strangelove.* He is in control of a Strategic Air Command (SAC) base and sends a wing of planes on a first attack on Russia. He explains his reason for doing this to his second in command, Commander Mandrake of the British Air Force, as follows.

RIPPER

War is too important to be left to the politicians. I can
no longer sit back and allow communist infiltration,
communist indoctrination, communist subversion
and the international communist conspiracy to
sap and impurify all of our precious bodily fluids.

He continues, after fighting off U. S. Army forces trying to stop him, and says the following to Mandrake:

RIPPER

Do you know when fluoridation began?

MANDRAKE

No. No I don't Jack.

RIPPER

Nineteen hundred and forty-six, 1946 Mandrake. How
does that coincide with your post war commie conspiracy?
Huh? It's incredibly obvious isn't it? Foreign substances
introduced into our precious bodily fluids without the
knowledge of the individual, certainly without any choice.
That's the way your hard-core commie works.

That is, of course, an exaggerated, ridiculous notion. No one could be that paranoid. Perhaps, but then we merely need to remember Senator Joseph McCarthy and the House Un-American Activities Committee or the reasoning behind the mere notion of anti-nuclear satellite missiles, and perhaps the ideas presented by General Ripper are not so far from reality. The diction in this piece takes a basic real-world notion and enlarges that notion through exaggeration. Because the notion is thus satirized, we first laugh at it and then later begin to think about the satirized version of the notion and the real world version. The diction makes us think about the main thought of the piece.

Plot in this genre will basically be linear and also has a fairly high degree of verisimilitude. This will primarily be true because the thought will be focused on social issues, and it is easier for the audience to make the connection between the piece and the real world if there is a fairly high degree of verisimilitude. Also, the plot will present a situation in which conflict can develop between two opposing forces or points of view. In *Dr. Strangelove* the plot is fairly simple, but it is based in a real world situation. The U. S. Air Force nuclear attack on Russia is a mistake. How can it be stopped? Or should it be stopped? From this basic premise comes a discussion of the main thought of the piece. In the end, all the planes but one are stopped. That plane drops a nuclear bomb, setting off the "doomsday device," and the world is destroyed. This is the "dark" ending that is typical of the genre. The plot in dark comedy serves an important function, setting up a premise in which the ideas can be explored comically and giving the audience a linear structure that creates the dramatic question, "What is going to happen next?"

The *characters* in the genre are primarily one-dimensional. They often represent one side or one facet of the social issue being satirized. In *Dr. Strangelove* the various facets of the military point of view are represented by several characters from the madman General Ripper, who represents the most extremely paranoid point of view, to Commander Mandrake, who represents a more reasonable, peaceful point of view. It must be noted, however, that Mandrake is a British officer. Director Kubrick seems to be saying that nowhere in the American military is there any sanity on this issue.

The characters are all stereotypes who contribute to the main thought of the piece. They not only are typed by what they say but also by their physical appearance. Perhaps the best example of this is the title character, *Dr. Strangelove*. He is a wheelchair bound, ex-German rocket scientist with a gloved right hand that occasionally flies out of control into a German Nazi salute. Dr. Strangelove is in charge of the U.S. nuclear rocket research program. It is he who decided the U.S. didn't need a "doomsday machine" because he didn't think the Russians had one.

He says the following to the Russian ambassador as they are both standing in the Pentagon war room with the U.S. president and all the U.S. military leaders watching an electronic map showing the SAC planes heading toward Russian targets.

DR. STRANGELOVE
The whole point of a doomsday machine is lost if you keep it a secret. Why didn't you tell the world?

He seems to be the maddest of all in terms of his physical appearance and vocal mannerisms. But, he also seems to be the only person who fully understands the potential for destruction inherent in the whole deterrent argument. Very often the physical mannerisms will add a degree of comedy and contribute to the one-dimensional aspect of the characters in this genre.

Spectacle will also have a high degree of verisimilitude in this genre and can help the audience see the correlation between the ideas presented in the piece and the real world. Spectacle can also be used to create physical humor. A portion of *Dr. Strangelove* focuses on the SAC B-52 and its crew, which gets through the Russian defenses and drops the bomb, triggering the "doomsday machine." The first time we see the plane is in the opening sequence of the film in which it is being fueled in the air by a large tanker aircraft. The interior of the plane and the operation of the plane are presented in what seems to be a very real world way. We see knobs, switches, and instruments and hear technical instructions that look and sound like the real thing. When we first meet the captain and the crew, they are flying a routine mission. The captain is dozing off while the plane is on automatic pilot. The crew are obviously bored and not paying much attention to their job, until the command comes through for the attack. The captain gets his top secret instructions, takes off his flying helmet and replaces it with a cowboy hat, and says in a deep southern accent the following:

CAPTAIN
Well, boys this is it. Nuclear combat. Toe to toe with the Ruskies.
(music under at this point)
If this turns out to be half as important as I think it might be, I'd say you all are in line for some personal promotion and personal citations when this thing is all over with. That goes for ever last one of you regardless of your race, color, or your creed. Now let's get this thing on the hump. We've got some flyin' to do.

The last time we see the captain is as the bomb is released from the plane. He is astride the nose of the bomb riding it toward the ground like a cowboy riding a bucking bronco. The war room and military base, which are the other two principal settings, also have a high degree of verisimilitude. The spectacle goes from real to ridiculous in many cases, which leads the audience to both laughter and to thinking about the ideas presented by the piece.

The *sound* in dark comedy also has a high degree of verisimilitude. In *Dr. Strangelove* the sounds of the B-52 and the battle scenes at the airbase are basically real world based and help create believability in the scenes.

Music plays an important satirical role in Dr. Strangelove as it often does in this genre. In the opening scene, as the B-52 is being refueled, the background music is the melody from the popular song, *Try A Little Tenderness*. When the captain of the plane makes his pep talk to his crew about the "Ruskies," the melody of the song, *When Johnny Comes Marching Home*, is played under the dialogue. Later that same song, along with a very military snare drum beat, is played as the plane is headed in to drop the bomb. The final shots of nuclear explosions representing the "doomsday machine" going off are accompanied by the song *We'll Meet Again*. In all of these cases the music accompanying the visual image creates the satirical effect that reinforces the ideas concerning the folly of nuclear weapons buildup and anti-nuclear devices presented in the piece.

By understanding the genre of a piece, one can more quickly understand the intent of the artists and be tuned in to how the dual purpose of art will be utlized. With this understanding, it should be more fun to watch the theatre arts.

PART TWO

THE ARTISTIC SIDE

Chapter 4

Criticism

The Audience as Critic

If there is such a thing as a critic, it is the audience. When you have that final ingredient-the audience-then you have the critic.
                                        Morgan Freeman, Actor[1]

Whenever we watch a theater arts performance, we make judgements about that performance. We talk about the piece with the person who went with us. Our friends ask us about how we liked the piece the next day. We all engage in the act of making judgements. We offer our own criticism. Thus, each and every audience member becomes a critic of sorts. Everybody who goes to the theater has the right to his own opinion, but he doesn't have the right to have it taken seriously.
                                        Tyrone Guthrie, Director[2]

The *key* to being a responsible audience member or a good critic is to *make valid judgments.* In order to make valid judgments as audience members, we must do and know certain things. An audience member must know the basic dramatic conventions of the medium in which the piece is presented to completely enjoy it and to validly criticize it. However, it is important to keep an open mind within the framework of these conventions. An open mind will allow us to experience the piece freshly and with as little personal bias as possible. The reality is that we all have biases. I don't particularly like musical comedy. You might hate horror films. The effective audience member is aware of those biases as he watches a piece and later criticizes it.

Once these basics are taken care of, then we can proceed to the following three questions.

Basic Questions of Criticism

1. What is the intent of the piece and the artists involved?
2. How well was it done?
3.. Was it worth doing?

These three questions and their answers are the core of effective valid criticism. *In order to answer these three questions an audience member must have knowledge of the art being criticized and a performance standard to which a given piece can be compared.* Both of these come with interest and experience.

The first question "What is the intent of the piece and the artists involved?" is fundamental to valid criticism. One must be able to analyze three basic concepts here. First of all, one must understand the genre of a piece. It would be invalid criticism to complain about the lack of depth of character in a film like *Ironman,* since the genre of *Ironman* is melodrama, and in melodrama characters will be one-dimensional. Second, one must also understand the intention of the piece, in terms of the dual purpose of art. If a piece is designed to be purely escapist entertainment then it is not valid to criticize the piece for not making us think. Finally, we must understand the intent of the piece in terms of whether it is supposed to be comic or serious or a combination of the two. If a situation comedy like *Three's Company* intends to make us laugh and we don't find it funny because of the sexist nature of the humor, we can validly criticize the piece because it doesn't make us laugh, but we can't criticize it because it wasn't serious enough.

The second question "How well was it done?" has to do with our judgment of the piece as a whole and of each of the various artists involved. In order to validly criticize at this level, one must have knowledge of what each artist does. In the following chapter the functions of the various artists will be discussed. The more we know about what each artist contributes to a piece the more we can appreciate it and the greater the validity of our criticism.

"How well was it done?" also has to do with comparison to other pieces like the one we are criticizing. If one has seen all of the Sylvester Stallone Rambo films, then one can compare them and more validly judge the effectiveness of one versus the other. Or, one could compare them to the war melodramas of John Wayne and make another, perhaps more valid kind of criticism. The more one has seen in order to set up a personal standard of "value," of "How well was it done?" and the more one knows of what each artist contributes to a piece, the more valid is the criticism.

The final question "Is it worth doing?" is the question with the broadest scope and concerns our own personal art theory. The theory should be based on knowledge and experience. One thing I want to make clear at this point, if you are an active audience member you must be open enough and flexible enough to realize that your basic ideas about art will be, and should be, constantly growing and changing.

An example of "Was it worth doing,?" could be the escapist entertainment television series, *Three's Company.* One could first of all object to the piece in terms of the idea that escapist entertainment isn't of any value. One could also object to the piece in terms of the overemphasis on sexist humor. This kind of sexist humor in a popular television show might suggest to some that sexism is acceptable. If either of these ideas seemed true, then the piece is not worth doing. On the other hand, if one thought escapist entertainment was valid, and maybe even necessary, in order to forget some of life's problems, and that *Three's Company* had humor that was very funny and harmless, then the piece would be very much worth doing. From this example, we can see that "Is it worth doing?" has a great deal to do with individual "standards" and "values" and one's ability to communicate them.

In all cases the key to valid criticism is having intelligent reasons for your judgments, both positive and negative. Remember that criticism does not mean finding fault. It simply means "the art of making judgments." As an audience member who can analyze and discuss critically, you will be able to engage in good lively conversation with your friends and give them valid reasons for your likes and dislikes in the theater arts. You'll be a more valued friend if you give them good advice about things they will enjoy seeing than if you are constantly telling them about the negative aspects of all the things you watch.

The Critic and the Audience

The critic can be important to an audience member as a consumer's guide for ideas about what to see and what not to see. But one can also read well-written criticism or watch a critic on television or listen to a critic on the radio and learn more about a particular art. Or, if the criticism is well written or produced it might by itself be a good read or interesting program to watch or listen to and thus is good art in and of itself.

As a consumer, it is important to rely on more than one critic. One should regularly read, watch, or hear several critics on a given piece and make a consumer judgment based on the opinion of several critics. It is extremely important, however, to know the likes and dislikes of each of the critics. Critics, like everybody else, have biases. Also, it is important to remember that professional critics are simply giving you their opinions. These opinions are perhaps more valid than your next-door neighbor's opinions because the critic is more of an expert. The key is that you need to have some experience with the critic's taste in order to trust his or her judgment. Also, a critic with whom you constantly disagree is as valid as one with whom you constantly agree. You simply do the opposite of what the one you disagree with tells you. If he says he loves a film, you know you'll probably dislike it. So don't go see it. This obviously takes some trial and error before you can figure out which critics work for you and which don't. But if you are going to use your viewing time, which is bound to be limited, to its best advantage, you need to use critics as a form of consumer guide.

Another benefit from enjoying criticism is that you can learn about a new art form at an elementary level through good criticism. I'll relate a personal experience to demonstrate this point. Several years ago I started reading architectural critic Benjamin Forgey in *The Washington Post*. I have no formal training in architecture, and at the time had only a passing interest, but I found his writing excellent and his description of what to look for in architecture very detailed and interesting. After a while I began to seek out buildings he wrote about. I would go to them and observe what he suggested was effective and ineffective in the building. Because of his writing I now have a greater appreciation of architecture and pay a great deal more attention to the art of buildings. Though I am only a novice, I have another art with which I can enrich my life. Good criticism gave this to me, and if you pay attention to good criticism in any art, it can do the same for you.

Critics and Reviewers

Criticism can not only be useful to the audience member, but oftentimes it is essential for the financial success of a film or a theater production. A good to "rave" review will bring in the audience. By the same token, a "pan" (a negative review) by a major critic in a city can mean very little audience and thus financial disaster, which can lead to a short run. Criticism can also be useful to the artists involved in a piece if it is valid and well thought out. "Compassion [for a critic] is almost, but not quite, as important as passion. Which is why critics must be careful when they make fun of people's physical appearance. It is occasionally legitimate, but there is a narrow line to be drawn between fair comment and needless abuse. An artist discouraged can be an artist lost." Clive Barnes, Critic[3] Artists can learn a great deal from good criticism. Though more often than not, artists dislike critics. "Asking a working actor what he thinks about critics is like asking a lamppost how it feels about dogs." Christopher Hampton, Actor[4] However, if the criticism is written by a critic whom artists respect and feel is knowledgeable and fair, the criticism will usually be considered valuable, even if it is negative. Actress Patrice Munsel said the following about critics with whom she has a problem: "I only resent a critic when, out of town, a sportswriter is assigned to review the show."[5] What she means, of course, is that the critic must know the art that he is criticizing in order that the criticism be valid. The audience should demand this of the critics they read as well.

The various sections of an effective piece of criticism will fall into one of three categories.

Categories of Critical Writing
1. Exposition
2. Appreciaiton/Condemnation
3.. Evaluation

Like exposition in a linear plot, exposition in criticism describes the background of a piece. Oftentimes the exposition in a review will, in fact, give the basic plot exposition of the piece being reviewed. In addition to that basic type of exposition, the review might also give background information of the artists involved, or productions in the past of the piece being reviewed, or the history of how the current production of the piece was put together. Any of this kind of information in a review would be called exposition.

Portions of a review that simply state likes and dislikes without any reasons for those likes and dislikes are called appreciation or condemnation. A reviewer might write a review that is a basic plot summary and then say in the final paragraph that he thought the piece was terrible. The following is a famous one-sentence review of condemnation: *Tallulah Bankhead barged down the Nile as Cleopatra last night—and sank!* The reviewer who spends 10 seconds on television reviewing a movie and then gives it "five popcorns" is simply doing appreciation and nothing more.

When criticism explains why something was or wasn't effective, its function is evaluation. The critic is then making a value judgment based on his knowledge and experience. It is at this level that judging theater arts becomes criticism and not just a review.

*The **reviewer** will employ exposition and appreciation and/or denouncement in the review. The **critic** will likely incorporate all three categories of criticism, with an emphasis on evaluation.*

One can take any review and analyze it in terms of the three categories of criticism. The following is an analysis a review of the play Thin Wall.

Paragraph #	Criticism Category
(1)	Evaluation

In Thin Wall, a punchy new comedy at New Playwrights theater, author Phoef Sutton looks at both sides of the veneer between our civilized selves and our violent primal urges.

(2)	Exposition

Duane wakes up in his friend Susan's Los Angeles

apartment and finds himself staring into the barrel of a
gun. It belongs to Matt, Susan's high-school boyfriend,
who has impulsively tracked her down eight years later to
make his long postponed sexual conquest.

(3) **Exposition**

While warily circling each other, Duane and Matt
overhear a domestic row: Susan's brawling neighbors,
thuggish Frank and his dim girlfriend, Pam, are going at it
on the other side of the apartment's thin wall. Matt tries to
break up their dispute. Outraged by this invasion of their
privacy, Frank and Pam rob Susan's apartment in revenge.
And so on in a spiraling chain of nastiness.

(4) **Evaluation**

Sutton suggests that Americans are awash in a numbing
wave of societal violence that can't help but seep into
our personal affairs. There is also more than a hint that
humans are innately attracted to violence. Though Duane,
a sensitive "new man" type [read wimp], is interested in
Susan, she is perversely attracted to Mr.. Wrong----the
boorish, physically overpowering Matt—who models his
black and white morality on Clint Eastwood.

(5) **Evaluation**

And though Pam has lost count of the times she's
been slapped around by Frank, she remains loyal with a
skewed logic that has her constantly apologizing to him
and everyone else, even defending his brutality. By play's
end, each of Sutton's characters has picked up the gun, and
each has confronted his attitude toward using force as a
solution.

(6) **Evaluation/Appreciation**

Sutton shuttles neatly back and forth between these
two odd couples, with Duane as witness and comic foil.
Though the situation is implausible at times, Sutton keeps
the verbal and physical tussles lively and clear, and his
curt, quick dialogue and sharp jokes about love and L. A.
have a funny, natural bite.

(7) **Evaluation/Appreciation**

Directed by Arthur Bartow, Thin Wall is competently
acted, with two standout performances. With his
constantly startled expression, Ernie Meier is an endearing
Duane, given to instant amateur analysis and deploying
a comic diplomacy when faced with a gun or a fist. As
Susan, Mary Woods is a wonderfully edgy career woman,
a seen it-all Mary Tyler Moore type who's having a
particularly bad day.

(8) **Exposition/Appreciation**

Playwright Sutton, who was born in Washington, is off
in L.A. writing sitcom teleplays. Though Thin Wall suffers
from more than a trace of television glibness, it also shows
Sutton's real promise as a playwright.

Written by Joe Brown[6]

Reviews are generally written in a standard format.

1. Opening paragraphs that will suggest the emphasis the critic will take in the review.
2. A basic plot summary.
3. Specific artists will be evaluated. This is usually the essence of the criticism. The area of emphasis discussed in the opening paragraphs will be dealt with in this section.
4. Closing paragraphs that will refer back to the opening in some way. General appreciation or denouncement will usually appear here.

Joe Brown's review of *Thin Wall* follows this basic format very closely. Paragraph (1) is very brief but makes it clear the review will emphasize the playwright and the ideas of the play. The plot is summarized in paragraphs (2) and (3). In paragraphs (4) and (5) Brown evaluates what he thinks is most important about this play, which are the ideas concerning inherent violence in American society. In paragraph (6) Brown continues his evaluation by discussing the merits of the playwriting. In paragraph (7) he talks of the director and actors with little detail but a great deal of appreciation. The final paragraph refers back to the playwright, which was part of the focus of the opening paragraph. In a limited amount of words, approximately 500, Brown has followed the basic format for writing criticism and has effectively explained his reasons for judgments he makes concerning this play.

Another basic way that critics approach a review is to focus on one particular element of a production. With this approach, the basic format concept is forgotten. The focus of a review will usually be on a major artist involved in the production, the writer, the director, or a "star" actor. Critic Paul Hume took this approach when he reviewed a production of the opera, *La Traviata*. Just to be certain the reader knew he was unhappy with this production, he titled it:

"Traviata Travesty, the Violation of Verdi's Violetta."

Violetta spread-eagled on a slowly revolving roulette wheel? Four caryatids holding up mirrored ceilings in all four scenes? An entire Traviata cast in chalk-white or off-gray makeup except for Alfredo? The women in the chorus looking like prostitutes in "The Rake's Progress"; the men looking as if they had dropped in from "The Boys in the Band?"
These are only some of the willful, gross distortions forced upon the Washington Opera's production of Verdi's touching masterpiece by designer-director Jean-Pierre Ponnelle. Easily the worst Traviata in my entire experience

(exceeding in bad tastelessness and violent distortion that of Visconti in Spoleto some years ago), it ruins much of the fine musical account.

It is essential to divide any review of this caricature into two parts, one discussing the revolting staging, the other the often excellent musical side. Ponnelle, whose perverseness wrecked "The Flying Dutchman" last season at the Metropolitan Opera, does have an inspired idea at the beginning of the Prelude. He shows Violetta moving slowly into the room of her Paris house where her party will soon be in full swing. As she lights twin candelabra on the supper table, she sees what looks like the deathhead of some sweet old nun, her face surrounded by the black and white wimple of her order. (Ponnelle says it is the corpse of Violetta, but don't you believe it!) As the prelude ends, Violetta covers up the waxy image with the tablecloth and proceeds to seat her guests around the table with its grisly little dish.

As the opening scene begins, the chorus, while singing, jiggles rapidly up and down in time to the music, looking exactly as if every one of them had forgotten to go to the bathroom before the curtain went up. It is perhaps the most absurd effect of the entire opera, one Ponnelle repeats with ever worsening result in what plays as Act III, though Verdi wrote it as Scene Two, Act II.

More minor damage is done during this $600,000 production (shared with the Houston Opera, where it originated) of Traviata than in any within memory: Two champagne glasses are smashed in Act One, a chair is overthrown in act Two, a table in Act Three, and a vase in Act Four. Quixotic lighting is marked by frequent, inexplicable, sudden white flashes. The roulette wheel appears in Flora's party. When Alfredo insults Violetta, throwing money in her face, it becomes the vehicle of her total disgrace in a scene that so horribly violates all of Verdi's thought and care for one of his favorite heroines that you have to think Ponnelle must hate La Traviata with a burning ferocity. Why else does Violetta suddenly become so ugly in the short time between leaving her country house and arriving at Flora's?

Perversions of equal violence continue right through the final scene. One of Verdi's master strokes, Violetta's reading of Germont's letter, which can be an infinitely touching moment with her dying voice over the solo violin, is wrecked by the director's conceit of having the voice of Germont read it over a loudspeaker! And still more: Violetta, feeble to the point of death, not only hears offstage revelers, they burst into her room and, dragging her from her bed, whirl her around! Friends, it is not to be believed.

What about the music? Much of it is lovely, headed by Catherine Malfitano in a role for which she had the classic look and a lyric capable of great appeal. Once past those treacherous shoals that end "Sempre libera," she is often impressive, making words count and spinning lovely quiet tones and ringing full voiced phrases. (But why no "g" at the beginning of "gioir," where it literally creates the mood intended?) With baritone Brent Ellis as Germont, Malfitano made the long garden scene the finest purely focal episode of the evening. Ellis sings handsomely and won a solid ovation. He ought to unbend toward Violetta at the end of the scene as Verdi indicates, rather than holding to his stony paternal rule.

Beniamino Prior's Alfredo was poorly sung with wavering pitch and unsteady rhythm. The chorus was excellent in song, fine in discipline, especially when you remember the awful thing they had to do.

Theo Alcantata conducted a strictly no-nonsense performance, refusing to stop for applause even after some of the most famous moments. In a way he matched the rigid manner of the staging. A touch more leeway for Violetta in "A fors e lui" would be welcome; a slightly more moderate pacing of the "Addio del passato" is necessary.

But when it was all over, the performance of Verdi's music was hard to recall because of the new meaning given to the vulgar and the cheap by the staging. How tragic![7]

Critic Hume leaves no doubt what the focus of this review will be. In the opening of the review he calls the director's work "willful, gross distortions," and in the closing tells us the director has given "new meanings to the vulgar and the cheap." With the exception of three paragraphs, which discuss the music, the remainder of the review details the reasons Hume denounces this production. To his credit Hume tells the reader of his bias against this director, "Ponnelle, whose perverseness wrecked *The Flying Dutchman* and of his bias toward a more traditional approach to *La Traviata*. This review is wonderful to read because it is so well-written, and critic Hume supports his judgments with delicious detail. From this review, one might be encouraged to go see this production if one liked the idea of experimentation in staging with basically well performed music. The focus in this review is its strength.

The theater arts need critics and obviously critics need theater arts or they have nothing to review. Effective criticism is important to the artists and to the audience, and while sometimes it may seem like a necessary evil, it is an integral part of the process of any performing art.

Chapter 5
The Artists

The Collaboration

The theater arts involve a number of artists collaborating to create a unified work of art. These two notions of unity and collaboration are essential to the success of any piece. Unity means very simply that all the artists are working together with the same goal in mind. In fact, sometimes an individual artist must forget about himself for the sake of the total production. In the production of *La Traviata* discussed in the previous chapter perhaps the director was too involved in his own clever staging to see that it disrupted the unity of the production. That is certainly the impression critic Hume had. In order to achieve this unity, all of the artists---the playwright, the director, the designers, and the actors--must work together. They must collaborate

The Writer

The idea for a piece generally begins with a writer and a script. The idea for a script will most often come from the writer. The writer will respond in some way to his life experience, his environment, and begin writing.

My plays are about myself and my friends.
George Bernard Shaw[1]

How long that will take and how the writer gets to a completed script has as many variations as there are writers. I write in bars and restaurants. At the start of the day I take my tablet and I go out and search for a play.
August Wilson[2]

I don't have enough ideas for a full-length play more than every few years.
Tom Stoppard[3]

It's my job as a playwright to hold up certain situations for inspection. People are too busy living their lives. I freeze some of the things they might have missed and run them back for them
Ron Milne[4]

Well, there's an old cowboy trick. The herd is coming through fast and one cowboy asks another how you estimate the number of cows so quickly. The other cowboy says: "It's very easy. You just count up the

*number of hooves and divide by four." That's how you write a play.
You do a lot of writing to figure out what the hell the play's about and
throw out three-quarters of it and write it again.*

David Mamet₅

What we can say for certain about a script is that the writer will respond in some way to his environment and put that response into a written form that is called *drama*. This written drama does not come to life until it is performed as a play or film or teleplay. This is why plays are done as readings and even to a degree why out-of- town tryouts take place before a play gets to New York. The playwright needs to see the play before he can be certain it will work. The film version of the out-of-town tryout is to show the film to a test audience and see how it reacts. Probably the most publicized version of this is the film *Fatal Attraction* and its changed ending. In television, pilots are done to see if the concept of a series will work. If it does, then a series is produced.

It is also very likely that the written work will go through many rewrites and that the end result may turn out far different from what the writer originally intended. This is even likely if the writer is working from a source other than his own imagination. Think of the times that you've seen a film version of a book you've read. Very often the film version is quite different from the book, sometimes even unrecognizable.

The writer of the theater arts must be able to write believable dialogue and to create a sense of what he expects in terms of the various aspects of spectacle. Also, the writer must understand the medium for which he is writing. Each of the three media requires a different approach from the writer, as well as a different format.

The theater generally relies more on dialogue than do film and television. The dialogue in theater will often be more poetic. Even though the characters may seem like real people, the diction of those characters will probably have a higher degree of imagery than in film and television. The writer for theater must understand the special nature of spectacle in theater and write with that understanding. If a playwright wants a high degree of verisimilitude in the spectacle, then he will probably have to limit his scenic requirements to one set. On the other hand, because of the convention of place in theater, the playwright can use various theatrical devices to suggest place and the audience will go along with it. The script example that follows is from the great American play *Death of a Salesman* by Arthur Miller.

Act I, Scene 1

*A melody is heard, played upon a flute. It is small and fine, telling of
grass and trees and the horizon. The curtain rises.
Before us is the Salesman's house. We are aware of towering, angular*

shapes behind it, surrounding it on all sides. Only the blue light of the sky falls upon the house and forestage; the surrounding area shows an angry glow of orange. As more light appears, we see a solid vault of apartment houses around the small, fragile-seeming home. An air of the dream clings to the place, a dream rising out of reality. The kitchen at center seems actual enough, for there is a kitchen table with three chairs, and a refrigerator. But no other fixtures are seen. At the back of the kitchen there is a draped entrance, which leads to the living-room. To the right of the kitchen, on a level raised two feet, is a bedroom furnished only with a brass bedstead and a straight chair. On a shelf over the bed a silver athletic trophy stands. A window opens onto the apartment house at the side.

Behind the kitchen, on a level raised six and a half feet, is the boys' bedroom, at present barely visible. Two beds are dimly seen, and at the back of the room a dormer window. (This bedroom is above the unseen living room.) At the left a stairway curves up to it from the kitchen.

The entire setting is wholly, or in some places, partially transparent. The roof-line of the house is one-dimensional; under and over it we see the apartment buildings. Before the house lies an apron, curving beyond the forestage into the orchestra.This forward area serves as the back yard as well as the locale of all Willy's imaginings and of his city scenes. Whenever the action is in the present the actors observe the imaginary wall-lines, entering the house only through its door at the left. But in scenes of the past, these boundaries are broken, and the characters enter or leave a room by stepping "through" a wall onto the forestage.

(From the right, WILLY LOMAN, the Salesman, enters, carrying two large sample cases. The flute plays on. He hears but is not aware of it. He is past sixty years of age, dressed quietly. Even as he crosses the stage to the doorway of the house, his exhaustion is apparent. He unlocks the door, comes into the kitchen, and thankfully lets his burden down, feeling the soreness of his palms. A word-sigh escapes his lips--it might be "Oh, boy, oh, boy." He closes the door, then carries his cases out into the living-room, through the draped kitchen doorway.)

LINDA, his wife, has stirred in her bed at the right. She gets out and puts on a robe, listening. Most often jovial, she has developed an iron repression of her exceptions to Willy's behavior–she more than loves him, she admires him, as though his mercurial nature, his temper, his massive dreams and little cruelties, served her only as sharp reminders of the turbulent longings within him, longings which she shares but lacks the temperament to utter and follow to their end.)

LINDA: (*hearing WILLY outside the bedroom, calls with some trepidation*) Willy!

WILLY: It's all right. I came back.

LINDA: Why? What happened? (slight pause) Did something happen, Willy?

WILLY: No, nothing happened.

LINDA: You didn't smash the car, did you?

WILLY: (*with casual irritation*) I said nothing happened. Didn't you hear me?

LINDA: Don't you feel well?

WILLY: I'm tired to death. (*The flute has faded away. He sits on the bed beside her, a little numb.*) I couldn't make it. I just couldn't make it, Linda.

LINDA: (*very carefully, delicately*) Where were you all day? You look terrible.

WILLY: I got as far as a little above Yonkers. I stopped for a cup of coffee. Maybe it was coffee.

LINDA: What?

WILLY: (*after a pause*) I suddenly couldn't drive any more. The car kept going off onto the shoulder, y'know?

LINDA: (*helpfully*) Oh. Maybe it was the steering again. I don't think Angelo knows the Studebaker.

WILLY: No, it's me. Suddenly I realize I'm going sixty miles an hour and I don't remember the last five minutes. I'm--I can't seen to--keep my mind to it.

LINDA: Maybe it's your glasses. You never went for new glasses.

WILLY: No, I see everything. I came back ten miles an hour. It took me nearly four hours from Yonkers.

LINDA: (*resigned*) Well, you'll have to take a rest, Willy, you can't continue this way.

WILLY: I just got back from Florida.

LINDA: But you didn't rest your mind. Your mind is overactive, and the mind is what counts, dear.

WILLY: I'll start out in the morning. Maybe I'll feel better in the morning.

(*She is taking off his shoes.*) These god damn arch supports are killing me.

LINDA: Take an aspirin. Should I get you an aspirin? It'll soothe you.

WILLY: (*with wonder*) I was driving along, you understand? And I was fine. I was even observing the scenery. You can imagine, me looking at scenery, on the road every week of my life. But it's so warm up there, Linda, the trees are so thick, and the sun is warm. I opened the windshield and just let the warm air bathe over me. And all of a sudden I'm goin' off the road! I'm tellin' ya, I absolutely forgot I was driving. If I'd gone the other way over the white line I might've killed somebody. So I went on again--and five minutes later I'm dreamin' again, and I nearly-(*He presses two fingers against his eyes.*) I have such thoughts, I have such strange thoughts.

LINDA: Willy, dear. Talk to them again. There's no reason why you can't work in New York.

WILLY: They don't need me in New York. I'm the New England man. I'm vital in New England.

LINDA: But you're sixty years old. They can't expect you to keep traveling every week.

WILLY: I'll have to send a wire to Portland. I'm supposed to see Brown and Morrison tomorrow morning at ten o'clock to show the line. Goddammit, I could sell them! (*He starts putting on his jacket.*)

LINDA (*taking the jacket from him*) Why don't you go down to the place tomorrow and tell Howard you've simply got to work in New York? You're too accommodating, dear.

WILLY: If old man Wagner was alive I'd a been in charge of New York now! That man was a prince, he was a masterful man. But that boy of his, that Howard, he don't appreciate. When I went north the first time, the Wagner Company didn't know where New England was!

LINDA: Why don't you tell those things to Howard, dear?

WILLY: (*encouraged*) I will, I definitely will.

Notice the detail that Miller gives concerning the set and that he specifically talks about, "a dream rising out of the reality." He then goes on to suggest how to achieve that feeling in the set design. He describes how the characters look in the initial stage direction, but from then on relies on his dialogue to establish everything else. Notice how much the characters tell us about themselves and their situation in just a few pages of dialogue. Also, in Willy's long speech about driving, notice how Miller creates the image of Willy's experience through the dialogue. In a film or teleplay we might actually see Willy doing this. The nature of the dialogue would then change as well as the nature of the experience for the audience.

Film and television are much more visually oriented, and the writer must write with this in mind. In the case of film, the screenwriter must give an impression of the image, of what the camera is doing at all times. This is done without a great deal of detail because the detail is left up to the director and the cinematographer. The dialogue in film will also generally be sparser and have a higher degree of verisimilitude than in theater.

The following is a primarily visual scene from the script for the short film *Leo and Mars.*

EXT. STREET NEAR ABANDONED SWIMMING POOL-DAY

A CONSTANT EERIE WIND blows through barren trees.
A tangled fence is in the foreground, LEO emerges
in the distance riding his BICYCLE with a makeshift
WOODEN CART attached to it. MARS is unconscious
in the cart. The camera follows them as Leo peddles out
of the frame. A torn sign which says "DANGER NO
ADMITTANCE" comes into view in the foreground.

FADE TO BLACK:

INT. WAREHOUSE GARAGE-DAY
It is very dark inside the warehouse. The only light glares
through the cracks and holes in the metal corrugated walls
of the building. Suddenly, a huge metal door start to open.
Leo is silhouetted by the glaring sunlight as he pushes the
doors open with both hands, his arms ending up spread
completely apart. He moves out of sight.

CUT TO:

The creaking sound of his bicycle is heard as he peddles it

with Mars in the cart into the warehouse garage area.

DISSOLVE TO:

INT. WAREHOUSE LIVING QUARTERS-DAY

A weathered skylight with BRIGHT GREY LIGHT seen through the dirty glass.

DISSOLVE TO:

Leo's living quarters inside the old run-down wooden warehouse. Oriental rugs cover the worn floors. There is a king size bed, a claw-foot bathtub, sink, kitchen table and chairs, a sofa with a leather recliner next to it. Both face an old TV set with the picture of a woman taped to the screen. Several MANIKINS are seated around the room. Candles are everywhere but the room is now lit by the grey daylight coming from the skylights in the warehouse ceiling.

DISSOLVE TO:

A 1950's table model TV sits on an old wooden end table facing a sofa with two female manikins dressed in fancy evening wear.

DISSOLVE TO:

A Formica kitchen table, circa 1950, with matching chrome chairs sits in one corner of the living area. In two of the chairs are female manikins.

DISSOLVE TO:

A king size bed made up with matching sheets and pillow cases. A female manikin in a nightgown is seated on the bed.

DISSOLVE TO:

A claw foot bathtub with a nude female manikin sitting in the tub.

DISSOLVE TO:

INT. WAREHOUSE GARAGE-DAY

Leo gets off the bicycle, moves to Mars and lifts her gently from the cart. He then carries her up the wooden stairs past a plastic covering and into the living quarters.

DISSOLVE TO:

INT. WAREHOUSE LIVING QUARTERS-DAY

Leo has put Mars, unconscious, in a leather recliner. Leo, in the foreground, is watching her closely as he attaches

a HANDCUFF to her wrist. The other end of the cuff
is attached to the arm of the chair. Leo than gets up and
walks away to another part of the room.

CUT TO:

Leo puts his outer protective grey jumpsuit on a coat
rack in the foreground. Mars is in the distance still in the
recliner. Leo moves toward her.

CUT TO:

Leo moves to the sofa and sits next to the female manikins
on his right looking at Mars who is to his left, unconscious
in the recliner. Her boots can be seen in the foreground
with chains around each ankle. Leo picks up a bottle of
coke, which sits on a TV tray between the sofa and the
recliner. He toasts Mars with the coke.

LEO
Welcome to my home.

Leo then sits back on the sofa, looks again at Mars, puts
has arm up on the back of the sofa and watches the blank
TV with the manikins.

FADE TO BLACK.

In contrast to the previous scene, which is predominately
visual, the following scene, from the short film *Call Krystal*, relies
primarily on dialogue.

INT. AMANDA'S APARTMENT. 3 AM

Amanda is sobbing in a darkened corner of her bedroom
with her phone in her lap.

AMANDA (V.O.)
I was terrified by that dream. The only person I could trust
was Georgia so I called her. She came over immediately.

CUT TO:

Amanda is sitting on the floor at the end her bed with
her arms around her knees, rocking slowly and sobbing.
Georgia, still has her coat on, and is making a drink for
both of them. She moves to the bed, puts Amanda's drink
on the floor next to her, throws her coat on the bed and sits.

GEORGIA
OK Mandy, what did this guy say?

AMANDA
(through her tears)
It's not just the one guy. It's all of them. Even the nice ones.
I'm suspicious of everyone now--the mailman, the grocery
clerk, even Alan, when he decides to call me.

GEORGIA
Honey, it's all pretend. Just a voice on the phone. They're
talking to Krystal.

AMANDA
No! I'm not Krystal! I'm Mandy. I can't stop thinking about
who they are. What they're like with their wives, their
mothers, their children.
(she pauses starts sobbing)
Why do so many of them want to hurt me?

Georgia moves onto the floor next to Amanda and puts her
arm around her.

GEORGIA
It's OK Mandy. They're just acting out. Better that they
pretend with you on the phone than do it for real. Isn't it?

AMANDA
(trying to stop crying)
I guess so.

GEORGIA
(she picks up the drink)
Drink this. It's Georgia's secret formula for curing the blues.

AMANDA
What is it?

GEORGIA
Cranberry juice and grain alcohol.

AMANDA
It sounds awful.

GEORGIA
Takes away your troubles and kills yeast infection at the
same time. It's gotten me through many a crisis.
(Amanda drinks and indicates she likes it)
Now let's see if we can't get you thinking nicer thoughts.

The two of the them toast each other, drink and slowly start another conversation.

AMANDA (V.O.)
We talked through most of that night.

FADE TO BLACK.

Notice how terse the dialogue is in these scripts and how the description gives us a clear sense of what we will see on the screen. These scripts were shot with one camera. This technique is called a "one-camera shoot." That means that only one camera was used for each shot with multiple takes of each shot. This technique allows for a great deal of flexibility in shooting, lighting, and editing, but also takes much longer than a multi-camera shoot. The one-camera shoot is the standard way most films and a great deal of narrative television are shot. The multi-camera shoot is used on television talk shows, sporting events, and some narrative television, specifically soap operas and some weekly series shot in front of live audiences.

The teleplay writer must understand the requirements of the multi-camera shoot. Generally speaking this type of television relies on interior sets that have a high degree of verisimilitude. The ability to write believable "real world" dialogue is important to narrative television because most of the action is talked about and not shown. That is not to say that believable dialogue is not important for film as well. Film generally has the advantage of higher budgets and longer shooting schedules which translates to more use of visual dramatic action to tell the story than television.

A writer must understand the advantages and limitations of each of the three theater arts and must tailor his script to fit the particular medium in which he is writing. A writer must understand the genre in which he is writing and know what his goals are in terms of the dual purpose of art.

The Audience and the Writer

The first thing we can look at when evaluating the writer is the *dialogue*. Does the dialogue seem *believable in the world created by the piece* for each of the characters? Is the dialogue *dramatically interesting*? Do we care about the characters and/or their situation? *Are our emotions aroused?* Do we laugh, cry, sympathize in the way the writer wanted us to? Obviously a positive response to all of these questions means the writer is doing an effective job with the dialogue, and more often than not, dialogue is key to effective writing in the theater arts.

Does the writer *understand the medium* in which he is writing? Occasionally one will see a play that would have been much better as a movie. This is a case of the writer not understanding the medium in which he is writing. On the other hand there are examples of excellent plays being adapted to excellent films by their writers. An example of this is the play *Driving Miss Daisy* by Alfred Uri. This play was excellently written and highly successful on Broadway and on a national tour. It was then even more successful as an Academy Award-winning film.

Another measure of effective writing is, if a piece is trying to instruct us, is it doing so within the context of the narrative or is the playwright's voice obvious when the message is being given us? *A good writer will stimulate our thought within the structure of his characters and plot and through effective dramatic action.* He will not preach at us to teach us. In fact, oftentimes it is long after we've experienced a good play or film or teleplay that we really begin to fully understand the meaning of the piece.

The writer in the theater arts is holding a mirror up to his society and his times. He reflects this image through his perception of that environment. That perception should be unique. Therefore, another measure of the work of the writer is *uniqueness.*

The best writing has *universal appeal.* This means the ideas and emotional appeal will stand the test of time. The comedy of Shakespeare's *A Midsummer Night's Dream* is still funny today some 400 years later. Universal appeal is probably the sternest measure of evaluation, but is the measure that separates the great writing from all the rest.

The Director

The director is often referred to as "the unifying artist." This means, at a certain level, that everything that happens in a production is a "directorial responsibility." One thing to point out at this point is that some of the directorial responsibilities discussed in this section are occasionally assumed by the producer. Directorial responsibilities can be divided into four basic periods of activity:

Theatre Terminology	Camera Arts Terminology
1. The Script Preparation Period	1. Preproduction
2. The Rehearsal Period	2. The Shoot
3. The Assembly Period	3. Post Production
4. The Presentation Period	4. Distribution

The director has multiple and varied responsibilities in each of these periods of development, and some of these responsibilities vary greatly depending on the medium in which the director is working.

The Script Preparation Period

The first step in the script preparation process is to acquire the script. The *optioning* of a script means that the rights to produce the script are obtained from the writer or his representative. This procedure is generally considered a responsibility of the producer and is discussed further in Chapter 6.

Once the director is given the script to work on, he must then analyze it. The *analysis* will begin with a general interpretation of the script in which the director will determine the meaning of the piece and the best approach to project that meaning to an audience. From the general interpretation the director will begin to focus on the more specific concerns of individual characterizations, style of acting required by the script, and style and/or period for the scenic, lighting, and costume designs, as well as any other design elements involved in the production of the piece. This will lead the director to discussions about his interpretation of the script with the designers involved in the production. The designers must understand the director's concept of style for the piece at this stage in order for the piece to have unity of style in its final form.

Many directors have a very "personal style" that we can recognize from one piece to the next. These types of director-stylists are often referred to as "auteurs" because they have such a strong hand in all of the elements of the film's production. Film directors from Alfred Hitchcock to Ingmar Bergman to Woody Allen to Spike Lee and Oliver Stone are all auteur directors. Their style is apparent in the design; the writing structure, since in many cases these directors write the scripts as well as direct; the mood; editing; and meaning of their films. It is particularly important for the director to be able to communicate his basic style concept to the designers so they can develop their design interpretation in terms of the basic style concept of the director. Generally the designs will go through several stages and a degree of change before they are finally approved and ready for the assembly period.

Once the director is comfortable with the interpretation of the play in terms of the characters, *casting* can take place. This is a very important step in the directorial process. *A director must be able to cast actors effectively.* If the wrong actor or actress is cast into a role, it is a very difficult if not impossible obstacle to overcome. A classic example of bad casting is the film production of *Taming of the Shrew* starring Elizabeth Taylor. Director Franco Zeffirelli did all he could to cover up a horrid performance, but it is obvious that he should have not cast Taylor in the first place. It is further obvious that Taylor came with her husband at the time, Richard Burton. They came as a team and the film would not have been made without the two of them together, so Zeffirelli tried to do the best he could with what he had. What he had was weak casting, and even a great director can't overcome that.

The final step in the script preparation period is the *paper blocking* of the script. This basically means *the planned movement of the actors on the set*. Directors generally do this in terms of shorthand movement notes in the script or with storyboards. It is at this point that the first major difference between directing for the theater and directing for the camera arts occurs. Theater directors basically concern themselves with the movement of actors from place to place on a relatively static set with some variety added through change in light intensity and color. The director of the camera arts, however, must not only be able to move the actors but must also be able to move the camera in relationship to the actors. This is a very important difference between the theater director and the film / television director. At this point in the planning of the paper blocking or storyboarding for a film or television production that is a one-camera shoot, the *director of photography* or *cinematographer* will often be brought in. The director of photography or "DP" is responsible for directing the camera and the lighting in order to produce the images the director is looking for. Because the DP and the director must work so closely together, it is very important that the DP understand the director's interpretation of the piece from early on in the production process.

Once the interpretation of the play, the design, the casting, and the blocking; called *pre-production* in the camera arts; are completed the piece is ready to move into the rehearsal period.

The Rehearsal Period

Though the director in each medium needs to be capable of making interpretation decisions based on that medium, from the rehearsal period on, the directorial responsibilities can vary greatly from the theater to the camera arts. For that reason the theater director and the camera arts director will be discussed separately in the remainder of this section. The one constant for all the theater arts is that the director works constantly as an editor of the work of all the other interpretive artists involved in the production.

The rehearsal period for the theater director is generally divided into four distinct sections. The first section is for *blocking* the actors. This involves giving the actors the paper blocking that the director prepared in the script preparation period. This is generally done in a

FISHING
Scene 3. At the lake.
(Narrator in spotlight) — *✗ to SL sit on Stool*

NARRATOR: During my second marriage in the summer my wife and I would spend time on a small lake in the mid-west in the middle of nowhere. She was the wife I loved. I call her my "real wife." One day we were coming back from town and a car we didn't know was parked at the locked gate to our lane. About a quarter of a mile down the lane we saw someone walking toward the cabin. We drove down to see who it was. It was Jackson.

Jackson from URC

REAL WIFE: *(Rushing up to Jackson and gives him a hug)* You might have called.

NARRATOR: She wasn't crazy about surprises but she liked him.

JACKSON: Annie left me so I decided I had better do some fishing.

— to left platform

REAL WIFE: Let's go down to the lake. *(She and Jackson move away to lake area. She gives him a fake punch in the arm, a kiss on the cheek and then moves away off stage. Jackson sits and picks up a fishing pole.)*

NARRATOR:He fished everyday the week he was with us but his heart wasn't in it. I'm not sure he even caught pan fish.

(Walt comes on moves to Jackson with a six pack and hands him one.)

Walt from URC to Jackson

NARRATOR:In the evening we would drink a lot, on the pier mostly, cheap local beer.

JACKSON: I'm so bummed I wrote again. You know how Nick Nolte paints like crazy in that Scorsese short movie when the blond won't do it with him anymore. He hears loud old rock and roll and paints.

(Walt nods and hands Jackson a beer)

That's how much I needed to write. Now you have to hear it.

Walt moves left to sit

(Jackson picks up a small spiral bound and reads. The poem he reads is scrolling on a screen)

"Leo and Mars"

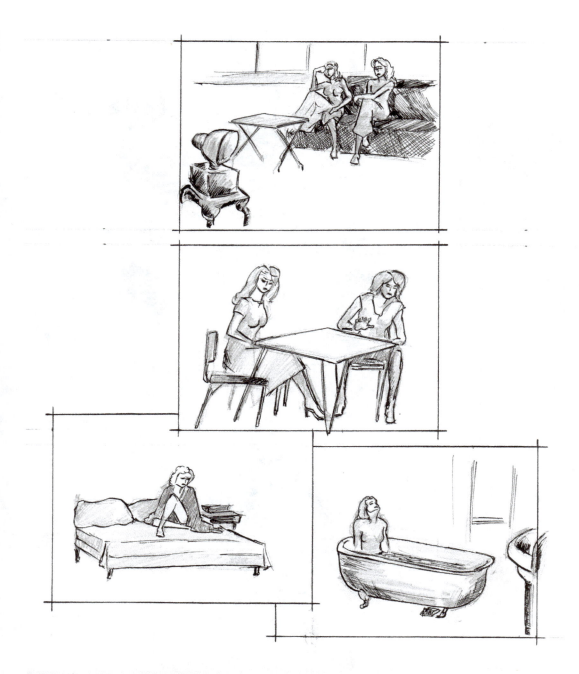

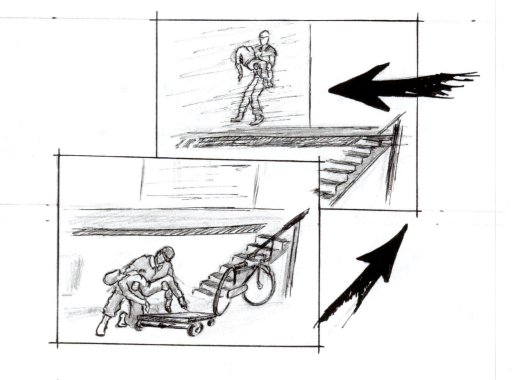

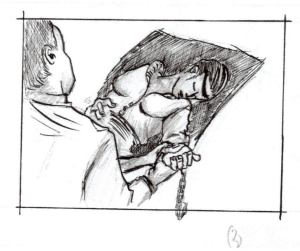

rehearsal hall with a "floor plan" of the set taped out, and rehearsal furniture instead of the actual set furniture. It is at this point that the theater director's chief assistant, the *stage manager,* starts working. The stage manager's main duties are to have the set and the actors ready to work at the beginning of the "call," or time the rehearsal is scheduled to start, to coordinate all calls with the director, and to keep track of all blocking changes as rehearsals continue. During the "run" of a production, or time the production is performed for an audience, the stage manager coordinates the cueing of all the technical aspects of the production and makes certain that the acting is maintained at the level rehearsed and set by the director.

Once the basic blocking, sometimes referred to as skeletal blocking, is set, then the *character analysis* section of rehearsal begins. The actors and the director will discuss the psychological make-up of the character and incorporate that into the skeletal blocking in order to begin to flesh the blocking out more so that the characters begin to come to life and the story of the play starts to take shape. The exact methods used to combine the blocking section and the character analysis section will vary depending on the director, the actors, and the play.

In fact, some directors will have the actors enter the *drop script section* before they begin to develop character. But obviously at some point the actors must learn their lines or "get off book." It is not until the actors have dropped script that the characters can fully come to life. It should be noted that in the theater, adherence to the script is very important. The goal of the director and actors is to perform the script as it was written and not to tamper with the words. If the script happens to be new and the writer is present for rehearsals, then the actors and director may ask for and sometimes even demand some changes in lines they don't feel are working or in scenes that don't seem effective. In the theater, with the exception of the new script, the words of the author are to be performed as written. "Actors accustomed to the theater know that the text is sacred." Ben Kingsley, Actor[6]

The *polish section* is the final portion of the rehearsal period. It is during this time that the actors can fine tune the characters they are playing. During the polish section the director will be doing *detailed editing of the actors. with the goal of setting the performance* so that it can be done consistently from performance to performance. The director looks carefully at the unity of the acting, and makes certain that what the actors are doing will work with the technical aspects of production, which will be added in the next step of the process.

The rehearsal period for the camera arts director may incorporate many of the same elements as the theater director rehearsal period. Generally speaking, the director of film or television will spend some time before the "shoot," the time the filming or videotaping is actually done, with the actors talking about character analysis. Many times, however, no rehearsal takes place before the actors actually come in to film or videotape. Therefore, when the camera arts director starts to work with the actors, they are expected to have their lines memorized and their character analyzed. Some camera arts directors will actually have theater type rehearsals with actors, but those are somewhat rare. The rehearsal will primarily take place on the set, at which point the director will "block" both the actor and the camera, run through that blocking a few times, and then shoot the scene. "Setting the performance" is not particularly important as it just has to be done once the "right" way and it is then captured forever on film or videotape. There is a bit more to it, but that will be discussed further in the one-camera shoot, assembly period section. The person who is equivalent to the stage manager in film is the assistant director, and in television the assistant director and the floor director share the stage manager's responsibilities.

The Assembly Period

The assembly period is considerably different for each of the three media of the theater arts. For the theater director it is a fairly specific but very complex final step before performing before an audience.

In the theater the assembly period usually takes a week to two weeks depending on how complex the design elements are. The actors have been rehearsed thoroughly and all the design elements—costumes, lights, sound, makeup, set, props, and maybe several others—have been planned and built. The assembly period is the time that all of these design elements come together and are rehearsed along with the actors. During this time the director divides his attention between the actors and the technical elements of production. There will be several rehearsals, called "technical rehearsals," devoted exclusively to integrating the technical design elements into the production. These will be followed by a series of final rehearsals, called "dress rehearsals," that are as close to performance level as possible. It is at this time that the director's ability to communicate with all of the other artists involved in production and create a unified whole is most important. Chaos can result if the director and the stage manager are not able to take control and successfully integrate all of the production elements by the time the first audience is sitting in the theater.

One of the major differences between directing for the theater and directing for the camera arts is the concept of *opening*. The deadlines are not usually quite so finite for the camera arts. One can usually push the opening day of testing the film or television pilot back a few days or weeks if the final stages of film or television assembly need to be delayed. The beginning of the presentation period can be adjusted a bit more easily for film or television than for theater. Once an opening has been scheduled for the theater, tickets will be sold and audiences will show up expecting a performance.

The *assembly period for film* involves two very distinct and important stages; *the shoot* or *production* and *editing* or *post–production*. Films and much of television are shot in what is called a "one-camera shoot." This means that with the exception of one-time events, like blowing up a building, the film is photographed entirely with one camera. The one-camera shoot principle allows the director and DP to have enormous flexibility in camera placement and lighting. The director can control exactly what the audience sees and thus the audience's viewpoint at all times when shooting with one camera. This concept is key to successful film directing. The major disadvantage to the one-camera shoot over a multi-camera shoot is that the one-camera shoot takes a great deal longer. But the flexibility and control of the lighting for one-camera shooting far outweighs any disadvantage.

At a certain level the one-camera shoot is equivalent to the technical rehearsals, dress rehearsals, and performances of theater all wrapped up into one and repeated every day and for every shot of an entire shooting period of a film. Every time the camera changes the angle of shooting a scene, the lighting, sound, makeup, set, and props designers and crew need to make adjustments. The film director, in his "paper blocking" and / or storyboarding, has to work out the number of ways he wants to shoot a single scene and work out what this means in terms of actor and camera movement. All of the design elements and the movement of the actors must match from shot to shot. This is called "matching action," and is key to maintaining continuity during the editing of the film. The better this is thought out in advance, the more likely it will work in the editing room, where the film is finally assembled. A major portion of technical rehearsal will obviously take place before the shot is finally filmed.

SHOT SCHEDULE

Shot 1: Master Shot Entire Scene
Shot 2: Over the shoulder shot, Actor A
Shot 3: Close-up, Actor A
Shot 4: Over the shoulder, shot Actor B
Shot 5: Close-up, Actor B
Shot 6: Extreme Close-up, Actor A-hands
Shot 7: Cutaway to Window as car passes by

On the preceding page is a simple example of the shot schedule for a very basic scene for a one-camera shoot. In this scene there are two actors, Actor A and Actor B. They are seated at a table.

Imagine that this scene is about 45 seconds long and consists of brief dialogue about Actor C. Shot 1 is an establishing or master shot that includes both actors and all of the set. It is a shot that can be referred to at any time during the scene but most likely would only be used at the opening of the scene and possibly at the end. The entire 45 seconds of the scene would be included in this shot. Shots 2 through 5 would also likely include all the dialogue. Though each

SHOT LOG

Shot 1:   Take 1-O.K.
               Take 2-No Good (NG)-Sound Problem
               Take 3-Good

Shot 2:   Take 1-Good
               Take 2-O.K.

Shot 3:   Take 1-O.K. One line messed up
               Take 2-Good

Shot 4:   Take 1-NG-lighting in camera
               Take 2-O.K.
               Take 3-Good

Shot 5:   Take 1-NG-glass in wrong hand
               Take 2-Good
               Take 3-O.K.

Shot 6:   Take 1-O.K.-line reading weak
               Take 2-Good

Shot 7:   Take 1-NG-crew shadow in shot
               Take 2-Good
               Take 3-Good

shot would focus on only one of the actors, the shot would provide reactions to what the other actor is saying in each case. Shots 6 and 7, because they are specialty shots, would likely only include specific portions of the dialogue. The director would have planned uses for each of these shots in his "blocked" script, but in order to have a wide range of flexibility and to make sure he got the best performance possible from each actor, he would likely overshoot in this manner. Also, the actor must repeat the performance of this scene for all of the first 5 shots. Therefore, it is important that the scene be somewhat "set" before the first shot through some rehearsal so that the actor can repeat in subsequent shots. The shot and "take" (a take is the number of times is shot is actually filmed) record might look like this:

So for this 45-second scene the director would have twelve O.K. to Good takes to edit from, and most of these takes are of the complete scene. This would allow for an enormous amount of flexibility when editing the scene. The person who would keep this shot record is called the continuity person and is also responsible for the continuity of action from one shot to the next. The director would give the continuity person notes on each take as it was shot. From these notes decisions would be made about what shots to actually print for use in the beginning of the editing stage.

When a film is being shot, the script will often change. Many times a screenwriter will be asked to write new dialogue while a scene is being shot. Because of this need for instant change, many film directors also try their hand at being writers. Many times the director will have a screen writing credit along with another writer as well as the directing credit. This very likely means the director did some writing and changing of the original script while shooting it. During "the shoot," all of the design elements are added, with the exception of most of the digital special effects. This means sets, lights, costumes, props, and makeup.

Once the film is shot, the second stage of the assembly process for film begins, the editing. At this point the director begins work with group of artists who are extremely important to the collaborative process, the editors. The *film editor* works with the director to select the best take from a given shot and arranges these shots to achieve the effect the director is looking for. They work with the script at this point but often make choices that deviate from the script. The dialogue will usually be close to the script, but the image might vary greatly. The film editor and the director "cut" the image and dialogue until they, and the producers, end up with what is call "picture lock." At this point, or sometimes as picture lock proceeds, a group of *sound editors* will begin to create the sound edit for the film. This means creating the "environmental sound" that reinforces the image and dialogue. Once this portion of editing is complete the final element of the film, music, will be added. Music is composed and edited to match the image, dialogue, and environmental sound. Often times all these elements are combined together in what is called "the final mix." The film director must coordinate the ideas and work of each of these people to produce the unified film that the director is looking for.

The *multi-camera shoot* is used for some narrative television productions that are produced in a studio. This concept of several cameras shooting the same event simultaneously is basic to live sports events and to live news programs. A director decides which of the cameras he wants "on-line" at what time and gives commands to the technical director who "switches" the production. This technique is used for most daytime soap operas and for situation comedies shot in a studio with a live audience. The director of these types of narrative television pieces plans the actor/camera blocking before the shoot as well as the camera that will be on-line at any given time.

The director's actor and camera blocking and the shot selections are rehearsed with the cameras first, then the cameras and the actors, then shot and switched while the scene is being performed. The concept here is to get it right the first time so that there need only be one take and no editing. The reality is that scenes often need to be re-shot, and separate takes can be edited together after the shooting has taken place. The basic reason that this method is used in soap operas is that it takes a great deal less time than does a single camera shot, both in the shooting and the editing. It rarely, unfortunately, produces work even close to the quality of the single camera shot.

The Presentation Period

The presentation period is the final period in the process. In the theater, this means the play goes in front of an audience and critics. A play will have several performances called "previews" before the critics are brought in. During the previews, the director will fine-tune all the elements of production. The actors will get notes about their performances. The technical aspects of production will also be adjusted. Lighting may change, a sound cue may need to be placed in a slightly different place, or a costume may need to be adjusted somewhat. In some cases, if the play is new, whole scenes will be dropped or rewritten. This is especially true if a play is headed to Broadway and the production is in an "out-of-town tryout." The director is looking at the overall production and working at unifying it so the play can be successful during performance.

Once the opening night has taken place, the director's work is finished. The stage manager takes over the production and the director moves on to other productions. The stage manager can call the director back for a rehearsal if he feels the show needs it, but beyond that the director's connection to a production that has opened and is running is simply to collect his royalties. With a little luck, the show will be a hit, and he will collect royalties for a long time and also direct road and international productions of the same show.

For the film director, the presentation stage begins with showing the film to a test audience. In many ways, these are like preview audiences for theater. If the film works with the audience, then it may be released in the version the test audiences saw the film. If it doesn't work, then some re-editing will be done. *Fatal Attraction* is an example of this process at work. In some cases the director will not have *final cut rights,* the right to the final edit of the film. Those rights may contractually belong to the producer. If this is the case, then the producer takes on that final directorial responsibility. Many times that is the case when major studios are producing a film with a new director.

Television does much the same thing as film in terms of trying out a piece in front of a test audience. They further extend this process with a pilot for a series by running it on the network during the summer and seeing what kind of ratings it gets. If the ratings are good enough, then the series will be aired in the next season. The director is not involved in this process in any way whatsoever. Once the piece has been shot and edited for television, the producer controls the piece. In most television series, the director will get a *first cut,* but the final cut will be left in the hands of the producer.

Although the specifics of the directors for the three media vary a great deal in some respects, the basic concept that the director is the unifying artist is a constant. The director more than any other single artist involved in the theater arts is responsible for the success of the production in terms of what the audience experiences.

The Audience and The Director

If a director is living up to his responsibility as the unifying artist, then, in theory, most of what happens in a production should fall under his control. Too often directors are given too much credit or too much blame for the success of a production. We can, obviously, separate certain kinds of outstanding individual achievement of other artists from the director's achievement. For instance, if a composer has written a great melody for a film that is obviously primarily to the composer's credit. Or if a designer has created beautiful costumes or fantastic animation sequences, then that designer has been particularly effective. At the same time, however, if these elements fit nicely into the whole of the production, then the director is to be credited. The converse is also true. If these special elements don't fit into the whole, the director is to be blamed. This is the first level at which we can judge the work of the director, the *unity of the production.* This is probably the simplest measure of success for a director. If all of the production elements work together as a whole, are unified, then the director has done that part of his job.

The area in which it is most difficult to judge the work of the director is the area of acting. Here again the concept of unity is important. If all of the actors are working in the same acting style and all the acting is of the same high quality, then the director is at least to get some of the credit. Obviously, the individual actor plays an important role in the success of each role. But it is the director who molds all of those individuals into a complete whole. There is a bit of a difference here between the theater and the camera arts. Oftentimes the theater is referred to as "the actors' art," and film and television are referred to "as the director's art." To some degree this is true. The actor in theater does have to perform the role every night and because of this the role changes a bit from performance to performance. In the camera arts, on the other hand, the actor's performance can be fine-tuned and in some cases changed greatly through the editing process. This editing process, as we know, is entirely in the hands of the director. But to a degree, the director of theater who has done his job has influenced the actor, and has "edited" the actor's performance during the rehearsal process. Therefore, the hand of a good director is very much present in the acting of a theater production as well as in the acting of television and film.

Casting is solely a directorial responsibility, though it is sometimes done by a producer, and therefore we can evaluate the director in terms of the effectiveness of the casting. Are all of the actors capable of playing the roles in which they have been cast? Does the cast work as an ensemble unit?

We can also evaluate the director in terms of the medium in which he or she is working. Does the director of theater know how to move actors on stage and incorporate the technical aspects of the theater with the actors' movement? Does the theater director understand the special "live" nature of theater and what this means in terms of the audience? The camera arts, of course, pose a whole different set of possibilities for the director in terms of movement of actors and camera, the use of spectacle and sound, and most importantly, the editing process. Does the camera arts director use these special elements of the camera to advantage? *Has the director used the medium to help create dramatic interest for the audience?* The director must use all the elements of the production to create dramatic interest or the director has not been successful.

This brings us to the two basic dramatic questions and the dual purpose of art. Can we understand what the director is trying to do in terms of these concepts, and has he been successful at it? This is a very important measure of the success or failure of the director. In order to judge this concept, we can also judge the use of genre by the director. *What genre is he working in and does he seem to understand it?* If it is a mixed genre, how successful is the mix? Let me add that many times a good director can be judged on not how he followed the basic genre pattern but rather on how he successfully and creatively varied the basic genre pattern.

Because of the importance of the director in the process of a production, we often judge the success of the piece based on the success of the director. Therefore, we must carefully evaluate all the elements of directorial responsibility to validly judge and appreciate the director's work and the piece as a whole.

The Actor

As an audience, our first level of response is obviously to the actors. They are the ones we see and hear, respond to, and with whom we identify. The actors are the big names, create the big headlines, and get the big money. Oddly enough most of the serious actors don't act for any of those reasons. They act because they have to. That's an odd thing about the whole artistic side of the theater arts. Once you've become involved and enjoyed that involvement you want and need to continue to do it over and over. Actress Mary Beth Hurt expresses this idea best.

> *I always wanted to act, especially when I realized that I could do it as a profession. Acting is like a sexual disease. You get it and you can't get rid of it.*[7]

Two other actors express it this way.

> *After studying acting for eight years, four of them at Julliard, I was fully prepared to be a waitress for the rest of my life, if that's what it took.*
> Kelly McGillus, Actress[8]

> *I don't regard two hours on-stage as work.*
> Sam Waterston, Actor[9]

Actors love what they do partly because they get to be another human being for a time. "You don't create a character on-stage, you create a human being," Robert Proskey, Actor.[10] This allows actors to express emotions that they may not be allowed to express or want to express in their real life. But as actress Kate Reid says, "Acting is not being emotional, but being able to express emotion."[11] That is an important distinction to understand. Being emotional means losing a degree of control. When actors express emotion, they are in control because they are doing it as a character and giving the impression to the audience that the emotion has verisimilitude. The actor accomplishes this through training and experience. Because the actor can express emotion, we the audience believe what the actor is doing and respond to and enjoy the performance.

Acting Training Systems

I'm luckily the product of two different traditions. There's the older tradition of the town crier. . . you get the line and say it loud and clear. It's theater from the outside, without too much introspection. But then I was in a production of "The World of Sholem Aleichem" with people who were familiar with a different tradition of acting. . . being true to your feelings and establishing the base of those feelings. It was there that I learned some of the interior things we should know about.
                              Ossie Davis, Actor [12]

In the statement above, actor Ossie Davis talks about the two basic approaches to acting that are used by actors and taught in actor training programs today.

The first approach that he mentions is often referred to as "technique acting." *The basic concept here is that you must be able to control the techniques of vocal production and bodily movement to convey the character to the audience.* Furthermore, the theory of this approach suggests that if an actor does the correct physical activities for an emotion, then interior understanding of that emotion will logically follow. This approach is also referred to as the "outside-in" approach to acting.

The second approach that Ossie Davis mentions is "method acting." A Russian director, named Constantin Stanislavsky, in the earlier part of the twentieth century developed this approach. Stanislavsky was the head of the Moscow Art Theater and realized that a new approach to acting was needed in order to effectively communicate the style presented by the new more "realistic" theater writing of the time. He was particularly concerned about doing justice to the writing of his fellow Russian and friend, Anton Chekov, the author of the Russian classics, *The Cherry Orchard* and *The Three Sisters,* among many others. Stanislavsky's approach was based on creating a look of verisimilitude on stage. He wanted actors to seem like real people, not orators, which was more or less the style of the time. To accomplish this, he had his actors work long and hard on the psychological make-up of the characters they were playing. The method approach comes at the character from the opposite direction of the technique approach. *The method actor works at understanding the emotional and psychological make-up of a character and then lets that understanding project itself physically.* This approach is also referred to as the "inside-out" approach to acting.

It is important to understand that Stanislavsky fully realized that an actor needs technical training. The Moscow Art Theater training program focused during the first two years on voice and body work. It was only after an actor mastered his technique that he went on to focus his attention on interior analysis of character.

Stanislavsky's most important contribution to the art of acting is the focus on character analysis. Because of his emphasis on the interior aspects of character, the majority of contemporary actors work to some degree on understanding the psychological make-up of the character they are playing.

At the simplest level of character analysis an actor looks at the "five W's." *Who* is the character? This involves basically the character's background and physical characteristics. *What* is the character doing? *Where* is the character doing it? *When* is the character doing it? *Why* is the character doing it? It is at this "why level" that the actor must work at understanding the emotions and psychology of the character.

For the actors who use a more complex level of character analysis the approach will divide a role into "character beats" or "motivational units" and assign an "objective" to each beat. The actor will further tie these beat objectives into a "through line of action" or "the major motivating force" of the character. Then the actor will develop a complete written biography of the character based on what the character does, what the character says, what other characters say about the character, the actor's own interpretation of the character, and the actor's imagination.

The degree of analysis will be individual for each actor, with the technique actor generally doing less detailed analysis than the method actor. But both types of actors will use some highly individual combination of both technique and method to create a believable character for the audience.

Acting for the Theater versus Acting for the Camera

In the theater you continue to improve your performance and when the run is over it's over forever and only stays in the memory of the actors and the audiences. But on film, where you don't have a chance for lengthy rehearsals and to fine hone your performance, it's there forever.
Jessica Tandy, Actress[13]

Actress Jessica Tandy touches on a major difference between theater acting and camera acting in this statement. *Each time the theater piece is performed it changes a bit and will not be repeated precisely that way again.* The interaction between the audience and the actors is different with each audience. Sometimes the differences are very minimal and the actors are doing primarily the same performance each time, but none-the-less the actor can work on subtleties that can fine-tune the performance in the theater. *In film the edited version is the final version and it will not change.*

Also as previously noted in the section on directing, the amount of rehearsal is usually much less for the camera arts than for the theater. For some actors this is difficult as they are used to setting their performances over an extended rehearsal period. Others welcome the spontaneity that the camera can capture and that perhaps they couldn't repeat. Jessica Tandy would seem to lean toward the theater approach, but it's hard to imagine a better performance than the one she gave in the film version of *Driving Miss Daisy*. Whatever the approach to rehearsal the director used, she is the consummate professional and adapted to the director's technique to produce a brilliant performance. Good actors must be able to adjust themselves to the approach of a director.

It has been said that *theater acting is energy* and *film acting is concentration*. What this means is that in theater once the curtain is up the actor must maintain the energy of the performance for the two to three hours it takes to complete that performance. The camera arts actor, on the other hand, must be able to sustain his or her concentration over a full day in order to be ready to play the character for the brief amount of time he will actually be performing before the camera. The reality of film acting is that most of the time is spent with the technical elements of production, the lights, sound, make-up, costumes, and cameras, adjusting from shot setup to shot setup. Furthermore, the film actor must be able to sustain this routine for several days and weeks and sometimes months depending on the shooting schedule of a film.

> *I always lose weight when I do a play. I gain weight when I do a film.*
> John Lithgow, Actor[14]

> *I don't understand why performers want to do movies or TV specials instead of performances. To me, making movies is about sitting in a trailer and eating doughnuts.*
> Jay Leno, Actor [15]

The "size of the performance" is another major difference between theater and the camera arts. *For the theater the actor must "project" his voice and his actions to the audience.* No matter how small the theater, this means enlarging the physical and vocal aspect of character to some degree. *In film, the actor does just the opposite. He must play the character small.* The camera is a very intimate observer. Many actors cannot make this adjustment from the live theater to the camera or vice versa. Many times the reason that they can only work in one medium has to do with the difference in need for the size of performance.

The relationship between the actor and the director in some ways is similar to and in some ways is different from the theater and the camera arts. In both cases the actor must trust the director to be an audience and to judge performance. However, in the case of the theater, once that audience arrives the actor then is on his own. Actor Alan Bates says it this way. "The thing I enjoy in the theater is that the actors are in charge of it. Once the curtain goes up, it's up to them."[16] Up until the audience arrives, during rehearsals, the director functions as the audience and edits what the actor is doing in terms of what the director wants from the character and how the actor interprets the character. The director is, of course, in charge.

It is the director's responsibility to see that each actor fits his or her interpretation of the individual character into the ensemble of the entire acting company. But the theater actor can sense that also, since at various points during the rehearsal process the entire piece will be run from beginning to end. In film it is entirely different. The actor must rely solely on the director as an audience. The actor might see the "dailies," the prints from the previous day's work. But it is unlikely that the actor will ever see the total shoot, because a particular actor is only around for the scenes in which he or she is involved. It is very difficult for the actor to judge the quality of his work for the camera arts until the film is edited. For that reason, the sense of ensemble must come to a large degree from the director.

The nature of each medium creates an enormous difference in approach for the actor. Film actors are not better than theater actors or vice versa. They simply require different techniques. If an actor is to be successful in more than one medium, he must understand these differences and adjust his performance accordingly.

Personality Acting versus Character Acting

Certain actors create a "persona" that they use on screen. They use this persona as the basis for all of the characters they play. Queen Latifah, Vin Diesel, and Melissa McCarthy are two of these actors who have made a career playing one basic character slightly adapted to each movie they are in. This type of acting is referred to as "personality acting." In film and television acting, particularly, this type of acting can be quite successful. The opposite of this is the "character actor" who works at creating a totally different character each time he or she does a role. Contemporary actors who are successful as character actors are Eddie Redmayne, Will Smith, and Cate Blanchette.

Many actors fall somewhere between these two extremes, using a large portion of their own personality and adapting it somewhat to the character. It is important to understand that all of these approaches require talent and technique and that one type is not inherently better than another.

Acting Style

Style in acting relates to two basic elements that are closely linked to one another. These elements are the size of the acting and the time period in which the piece takes place. The director will establish these two elements of style.

As previously discussed, the size of the performance will be in some ways determined by the medium itself. But in addition to this inherent size difference, there are further variations. All one has to do is to think of the difference between the acting in the television series *Black-ish* versus *Game of Thrones*. The basic acting difference here is one of size, which greatly determines the style. Imagine how out of place and unbelievable a character from an episode of *Black-ish* would seem on *Game of Thrones*. In *Black-ish* the physical acting is exaggerated, larger than life, and the lines are "punched up" for laughs. In *Game of Thrones* the acting is more subdued, more life-like. The characters behave more as real people in those same situations would.

The "historical time period" in which a piece takes place can also have a great effect on acting style. It is hard to imagine doing a play like Christopher Hampton's *Les Liaisons Dangereuse* without suggesting the style of the eighteenth–century French aristocrats presented in the play. Because of the way the characters dressed and walked and talked and because of their social mores and customs, a "period style" can be inherent in a piece.

An actor must understand the style of the production and do all he can to adhere to that style in order that unity is achieved through ensemble acting.

The Audience and The Actor

If you're caught acting, nobody believes you.
Lillian Gish, Actress[17]

The first and most important area in which we can judge an actor is *believability*. If we can't believe the actor as the character, then the acting is simply not successful. Believability relies on several other elements of acting that we can evaluate. The *acting must be fresh*. This simply means that the actor must make us believe that what he is doing is happening for the first time. He must help *create for us the illusion of the first time*. In order for this illusion to work, the actor's technique must not show. We don't want to see the actor pausing for laughter or getting ready to be hit by a "breakaway" chair. The actor must *maintain control*. That is to say, though the character may be emotional, we do not want to feel that the actor is not in control of that character's emotion. The actor must convince us that his physical build and voice are appropriate for the role. If the actor has all of these various elements of technique under control, the audience will, more than likely, believe the character.

The actor must also *work as part of the ensemble,* must contribute to the unity of the production. This means that the actor must be working in the same style and size as the rest of the cast. This is a shared responsibility between the actor and the director, particularly in the theater.

The audience must believe the characters in order to believe the production. If we don't believe the characters, we will not enjoy the production and our emotions wouldn't be aroused or our thought stimulated.

The Designers

The general audience probably knows the least about the work of the designers and their contribution to a piece. But oddly enough an audience would instantly criticize a mistake in design. If the lighting is inadequate in the theater, it is immediately obvious because the audience can't see the actors. If the action of a film takes place in the past and an actor is wearing shoes from the present, the audience instantly objects and stops believing. We expect from the designers a high level of expertise and craft because they have given us so much in terms of spectacle, sound, music, and special effects.

Designers in most areas of the theater arts have to be an interesting combination of artist and craftsman. They have to be able to communicate to a director their ideas at the earliest stages of design development. Once these ideas are approved by the director, the designer must turn them into very technical drawings in order that the design can be constructed. Once the construction is done many of the designers then must execute the finishing touches to the design.

The Basic Design Approach

Though the details of design can vary from designer to designer, basically the design goes through three stages. The first stage is the interpretation and preparation stage. Like the director, the designer will read the script and try to find a way to communicate the ideas and mood of the script through the design. Each designer, however, must incorporate the director's interpretation into the design concept in order to maintain the unity of the production.

The designer must understand the basic "style" concept that the director wishes to use in a piece. One level of style will be concerned with the historic time period in which the piece takes place. This is referred to as period style. If a piece is after complete verisimilitude, then the design elements must be historically accurate. In the *Godfather* films, for instance, as the films progressed from decade to decade, the clothes, hairstyles, cars, furniture, and other elements of spectacle, sound, and music all were historically accurate in terms of period style.

However, many times a director wants to deviate from period style accuracy and emphasize some specific elements of a historical time period for the sake of mood or aesthetics or simply create a world that is stylistically different from our own. This is called "stylization." We can look at two different films to see this concept at work. In the Warren Beatty production of *Dick Tracy*, he took a basic period style from the 1930's and had his designers exaggerate elements of the period style to create a "stylized" version of the time period. Director Terry Gilliam's designers created a "stylized" world in his film *Brazil* that incorporated various elements from several different time periods of our real world with fantasy world design elements. In both of these films the design "stylization" contributed to the overall mood of the film.

The designer's first ideas will come in some basic elementary form. For the set designer, costume designer, special effects designers, and some of the other designers, this form will often be a series of thumbnail sketches. Below is a thumbnail sketch by designer Chuck Vaughan for a production of *Coming Attractions* by Ted Tally that was produced by the Washington Theater Wing. The important thing about these sketches is that they communicate the design concept to the director.

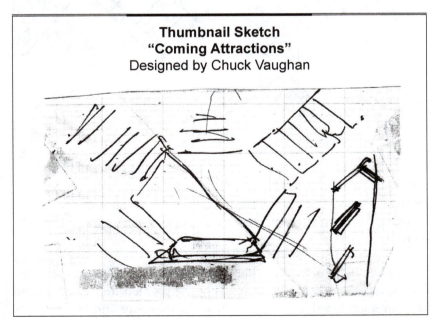

**Thumbnail Sketch
"Coming Attractions"
Designed by Chuck Vaughan**

It is very important that a director understand the language of the designer in order to understand what the designer is suggesting. In fact, at times directors and designers simply can talk through design ideas and skip the initial drawing stage. This can save a lot of time and energy. Once a director finds designers with whom he can communicate and whose work he likes, they will work together over and over. The work following the sketches will usually be more formal drawings or models, or detailed written notes relating to the script in the case of non-visual design such as sound.

Once the finalized version of the design is approved, then the designer must create drawings for the construction stage of the design. At this point the designer must work with many practical considerations including budget, materials, method of construction, safety, and other factors that vary with the needs of a particular production. A very simple construction drawing for the Vaughan set follows:

During the construction stage, the designer will be working with

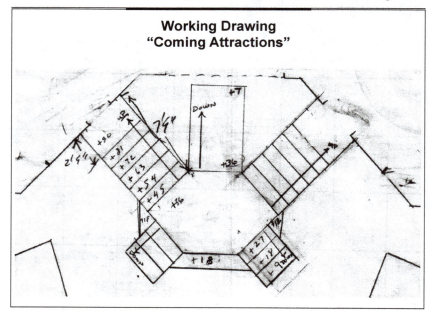

**Working Drawing
"Coming Attractions"**

a variety of specialized craftsmen and technicians with whom he must also be able to communicate. In some areas such as sound, the designer will often be the single craftsman, or one of the craftsmen, as well.

After the design is constructed, the completion of the design takes place in the artistic finalization stage of the design. This means, for example, in theater, that the sets are painted and dressed, the costumes are fitted and ornamented, the make-up and hair or wigs are applied and fitted, the lights are focused, colored, and cued, and the sound and music are cued. In film the sets, costumes, make-up, and lights are all in this stage at the time of the shoot. However, several design elements are not completed until the film goes into "post production" (the time after the major shooting is done and during which editing takes place). Many special effects and sound and music don't reach this finalization stage until "post."

Though the basic approach to the design process is the same for most designers and for all the media, designers tend to work in only one area of design such, as a set designer or a lighting designer, and within one medium. The designer, like the director, must understand the special qualities of each medium and design for that medium.

The Audience and the Designer

The first measure of any element of design is *unity*. Does the design fit into the whole of the production? No design element should call attention to itself unless that attention is designed into the overall unified concept of the production.

The second measure of the design has to do with the *aesthetics of the design*. Are the color, line, and balance of the design appropriate to the production? Do the aesthetics of the design help create the world of the piece? Do the aesthetics fit the overall mood of the piece?

The third and final measure of the design has to do with the *unity of mood*. Does the design element fit into the mood style of the production? Does the design element help to convey the general comic or serious style of the piece?

Design can add a great deal to the overall success of a production and contribute greatly to the level of believability for the audience

PART THREE

THE BUSINESS SIDE

Chapter 6

The Producer

Show Business

Someone once said, probably in defense of a vapid escapist Broadway musical, that theater art is called "show business" not "show art." However, a piece can be good art and good business at the same time, the concept here being that the theater arts need a great deal of money to mount a production, and that production can generate a great deal of income or profit. It falls within the duties of the producer to find that money, to allocate it, and then to divide the profits or minimize the losses. *The producer controls the business side of show business.* However, the producer, because he or she controls the purse strings, can and usually does have a large measure of artistic input. The producer does the hiring and the firing, and this applies to the person who is normally in charge of the artistic input, the director, as well as anyone else. If a producer like Steven Spielberg decides to produce a movie that he will have someone else direct, you can bet that Spielberg is in control artistically. A case in point is the film *Gremlins* which is credited as "A Steven Spielberg Film" but was directed by Joe Dante. This means that Spielberg produced the film and assumed many of the directing responsibilities in the "post production" stages.

To define exactly what a producer does is very difficult because the duties assumed by a producer can be so varied. Charles Fleming, in a article in *American Film* points out that even the Producer's Guild of America cannot come up with an adequate set of guidelines to use when deciding who is or isn't a producer or what is the difference between an executive producer, associate producer, or supervising producer. He points to the following as part of the problem. "In 1983, when the PGA tried to become a union, the National Labor Relations Board ruled that producers can't be a union, because their jobs are essentially management."[1]

"Management" is the key term here. Producing responsibilities are primarily those of management, specifically, management of money and people to produce a piece of theater or film or television. This is the principal responsibility of the producer.

The Duties of the Producer

The first management responsibility of the producer is to find and develop the script. The script is the centerpiece of what is often called "the project." A producer will *option* a script or story idea from a writer. Many times the story idea will be in the form of a novel, short story, play, or even just a "treatment" of a script, which presents the basic plot line and characters. *An option means that the producer agrees to try to develop the project into a finished product within a specified length of time.* For that, the writer is paid a fee and possibly a percentage of the profits. The producer will usually make these arrangements through the writer's agent.

The *agent* represents the writer and thus works for the writer in the sense that the agent's job is to sell the writer's script to the highest bidder. For this the agent receives 10 to 15 percent of the writer's fee. In 1990 two agents more than earned their keep when one negotiated a fee of $1.75 million for Shane Black's *The Last Boy Scout* and another agent negotiated a fee of $3 million for Joe Eszterhas's *Basic Instinct*. On the other side of the coin Steven Spielberg paid three eighth graders $250 for a storybook style script they submitted to him. Needless to say these three examples are not typical amounts for a script. The Dramatists Guild and The Writers Guild establish minimums for scripts within each of the media, and the bargaining usually starts at the level of those minimums for Guild members as well as nonmembers.

Once a producer has "optioned" a script, he will begin to raise the money to produce the script. This might mean lining up a cast of "stars" and a "name" director to help sell the project to potential investors, or it might mean simply "shopping" the script on its own. In either case, the producer will have to negotiate contracts with a director's agent and actor's agents somewhere along the line. This will, obviously, have an impact on the bottom line. Once that bottom line is established and the producer has raised the money for the piece, then the producer's responsibilities become more specific to the particular medium. For that reason, the following discussion will deal specifically with the theater producer and the camera arts producer.

The producer of theater, though concerned with the artistic aspect of production, will tend to leave that primarily to the director. A theater producer will look at an occasional run-through of a production during rehearsals but generally will be only concerned with any suggested major changes in the script or technical aspects of production. If, on the other hand, during final rehearsals or early performances of a production the show doesn't seem to be working, then a producer will often become very concerned with finding a way to make the show work artistically. This can include making suggestions about the direction of a production or even replacing the director. *However, the theater producer's primary responsibilities are concerned with the business of the production.* The producer negotiates all union contracts. For a Broadway production this can mean more than ten different unions, from ushers to actors to stagehands. The producer and his company manager and / or production manager are responsible for getting rehearsal space, renting the theater, making sure the sets, costumes, lights, props–all the technical elements of production--are built on schedule within the budget and delivered on time to the theater. The press agent or public relations director is in charge of publicity and advertising. The box office must be available for ticket sales. The business manager must do a weekly payroll. All of these are theatrical producer responsibilities.

The theater producer will stay with the play as long as it runs in the production that his or her company is producing. In some cases this can mean years if the piece is a smash Broadway hit. However, at some point the producer will turn the "running" of the show over to the business manager and company manager in much the same way the director turns the show over to the stage manager. The producer is then free to move on to producing another project while the previous one continues to generate income for the production company and its investors.

The camera arts producer oftentimes has more input into the artistic side of production than does the theater producer. This is in part due to tradition in both media. Though both the film producer and the theater producer will have approval and input in the casting stage, the film producer will often get the cast lined up at the same time or before the director is set. In some cases a film "star" will have director approval. Because stars for a film can be essential to its box office success, the producer will very often be more concerned with the star actor than with the director. Of course, in a handful of cases this can also be said of directors. But the simple fact is that the general public is much more aware of actors as stars than directors as stars. This is why many directors also produce their own films. They then have the final control, the purse string control, that comes along with the producing credit. The producer who arranges all of the initial developmental aspects of the project (the script, the stars, and the director, as well as the financing) is often referred to as the *executive producer.*

Once this stage of the production is set, then a *line producer* will often take over the film production. The line producer along, with the production manager, then sets up all the details for the shoot of the film and will be on location with the film as it is shot. The line producer's responsibilities are concerned with the day-to-day budgeting and scheduling so that the director and designers can accomplish their artistic goals during the shoot. The line producer will of course be in touch with the executive producer on a regular basis, in most cases, in fact, on a daily basis. The executive producer may well be looking at the "dailies," the shots from each day's shoot as they come in to be processed and work-printed, and talking with the director, the editor, and the line producer about the quality of those dailies.

In a major studio situation, the executive producer may have several projects going at one time. If so, an *associate producer* will likely be overseeing the line producer from the home office. This is where the demarcation of responsibilities begins to be hazy. Which producer does what will vary from film to film and from production company to production company. But the producers regardless of the title given to the various individuals involved must accomplish all of the above duties.

Once a film is shot and the editing process begins, the producer can have varying degrees of input. Generally, any director will have at least "first cut rights." This means that the director and the editor will edit the film as per the director's instructions initially. This first cut will then be looked at with the producer. At this point the producer will respond and a discussion will take place about what works and what doesn't work, what changes can be made, and sometimes what re-shooting has to be done. Several more "cuts" will then be made with or without the director, depending on the director's contract. The last edit is called the "fine edit" or "final cut." Here is where the producer can really take control. Many producers maintain final cut rights. This means they control the fine edit. Since editing is a key directorial responsibility, the person with "final cut rights" has a great deal of directorial input whether that person is called a director or a producer.

The 1962 film *Lawrence of Arabia* is an excellent example of how final cut rights can change a film. The final version of the film that director David Lean handed to producer Sam Spiegel was 222 minutes long. Spiegel wanted the film released as soon as he saw it but insisted than 20 minutes be cut out. Lean quickly cut out ten minutes and Speigel then cut out ten minutes more without a "fine cut" made by director Lean, who was never satisfied with the 202 minute version. In the mid it was decided to do the fine cut that Director Lean wanted.

> *Bob Harris, who supervised the restoration, began work on "Lawrence" by researching and then reassembling the original version. The soundtrack for the dropped twenty minutes had disappeared, so the principal actors (Peter O'Toole, Omar Sharif, Alec Guinness, Anthony Quinn, and Arthur Kennedy), all still alive a quarter of a century after "Lawrence" was filmed, were summoned to re-record bits of dialogue (some 30 lines in all).a negative needed to be repaired splice by splice; patches of missing footage had to be reconstructed out of trims and outtakes, and new sound made up to match it. In the end, Harris*

reinstated everything, bringing the film to 223 minutes. At that point-in April 1988–Lean and his original editor, Anne Coates, worked on the film for two and a half weeks, re-editing a couple of scenes that had never worked in any version and at last making their final cut. The restored Lawrence of Arabia now stands at 228 minutes.[2]

Bob Harris in this case functioned as a producer in his efforts to get this great film edited as the director had originally intended. It was re-released in 1989 somewhat successfully and is now available on DVD in the newly edited version completed in 2003.

This brings us to the final major responsibility of the film producer, and that is distribution. Very often the distribution deal for a film is settled in the early stages of the project. Distribution simply means getting the film out to theaters so that the public can see it and the film can begin to make back its investment. Distribution for the television executive producer means finding a network or individual stations to broadcast a piece. If the piece is a series, that will usually mean a "pilot," which will then be picked up if successful for a given number of weeks in a season. In order to be a successful producer in any medium one must pay back investors and make a profit. This is the business side of show business.

Theatre Business Structure

Because New York City has been the center of theater for so long, the way that most theater people and the theater unions think of theater business is based on the structure of theater in "The City." This structure is primarily three-tiered and labeled in the following way: *Broadway, Off-Broadway* and *Off-Off Broadway*. These same three categories can be seen in the structure of theater in most major cities throughout the country. By way of example, theater structure in the Washington, D. C. Metropolitan area will be compared to the theater structure in New York.

Today the Broadway theater has almost become synonymous with the big budget musical. Critic David Richards put it this way: "As an arena for serious plays probing timely issues, Broadway tends to be on a par with your average amusement park. Gut thrills are the order of the day, and the blockbuster hits have much in common with those daredevil rides that propel the customer through a series of heart-clutching loop-de loops."[3] The average musical on Broadway costs five to seven million dollars to produce. For that reason ticket prices can be as high as $400 a piece. Broadway producers cannot be risk takers because of the high cost of productions. In a Broadway theater a piece must run for at least two years to pay back its investors.

The actors union, Actors Equity, is typical of the unions that producers must work with in a Broadway theater. This union sets its highest minimum for Broadway theaters at $1,807 per week. Equity makes its distinction concerning what constitutes a Broadway theater based on the number of seats in the house. Any theater that seats more than 499 is considered a Broadway theater. The union's reasoning here is that a large number of seats means a larger potential income for the producer and thus more money to pay the actors. The other dozen or so unions that a producer must deal with follow this same logic, which contributes to the high cost of producing a show on Broadway and thus the low-risk mentality among Broadway producers. If a nonmusical production does get to Broadway it must have selling power, which generally means a name author or name stars who will bring people to the theater.

A recent look at the theater listings in New York City out of sixty-two Broadway and Off-Broadway theaters, forty-four had musicals in production and the other eighteen had non-musicals. The musicals include the long running *The Book of Mormon*, *The Lion King*, and *Phantom of the Opera*. The straight plays included *The Curious Incident of the Dog in the Night-Time* and *The Cherry Orchard*.

The Washington equivalents to the Broadway theater are the Kennedy Center's Eisenhower Theater and The Opera House, The National Theater, The Warner Theater, and Wolf Trap. These theaters also deal with a varying number of professional theater unions, though generally speaking not quite as many as the New York theaters. For this reason it is somewhat less expensive to produce theater in Broadway-type theaters outside of New York. The Broadway type theaters outside of New York City will tend to have two kinds of productions. They will either have "road companies" of shows that have been hits on Broadway or shows that are in "out-of-town tryouts" prior to going to Broadway. The runs of both of these types of productions will tend to be limited to a few weeks in the case of the "tryout" to several months for the "road show." The producers in this case will generally be from New York and will set up a multiple-city tour of the show coming from or heading into New York. Occasionally a theater like the Kennedy Center will originate a production. If that production is successful, it will go into New York on Broadway.

Professionally operated theaters, whether they are in New York or "out of town," will have theater managers. These managers "book" productions into their theaters. This means that a theater producer will arrange to have a production in a given theater, and as payment the theater management receives a rental fee and/or a royalty from the box office. Generally speaking the theater management runs the box office with oversight by the producer's business manager.

The Broadway theater is very high-risk for venture capital because of the complexities of producing on Broadway, but the reward can also be very high if a producer puts together a blockbuster success that runs for years on Broadway and tours the country and the world with spin-off road show companies. The theatre production of *The Phantom of the Opera* has grossed more than $5.6 billion at the box office worldwide according to its producers.₅

The smaller union theaters that exist in New York are referred to as *Off-Broadway*. Actors Equity starts this level of theater at 100 seats, and it goes up to 499 seats. There is a five-tier minimum salary structure starting at $566 per week and going to $1008 per week. The Off-Broadway producer must deal with fewer unions, usually only those for theater technicians, musicians, and designers. This can vary greatly from theater to theater, however. Because of this the cost of producing in an Off-Broadway theater is greatly reduced. Thus, the Off-Broadway theater producer can take more risks in terms of the types of shows that can be done. Most of the serious nonmusical theater done today is done Off-Broadway. Though even Off-Broadway, the writer, director, and/or the actors must have some name recognition to the theater going public in order for a producer to mount a production. Though the risk is less than on Broadway because the investment is less, the chances of making back that investment back is still very low. Because of this fact, if a show becomes successful in a smaller Off-Broadway house it will very often be moved to a larger house or even to Broadway in order that the producer can have a larger number of people see the show and thus generate a larger profit.

The Washington Off-Broadway equivalents are Arena Stage, The Shakespeare Theater, Signature Theater, Studio Theater, Woolly Mammoth Theater, and The Round House Theater. These theaters in many ways are like the New York Off-Broadway theaters but in one principal way they are different. All these Washington theaters are theater companies and most are resident theater companies. *A **theater company** generally produces and manages its own theater and plans an entire "season" of productions for that theater. The **resident theater company** also has a group of actors who work with the company for the season or a large portion of the season.* These types of theater companies also exist in New York but are the heart of the Off-Broadway theater movement outside of New York. The actors union, in fact, has a special resident theater contract that has a lower minimum that does a normal Off-Broadway contract because the actor is guaranteed a number weeks of employment, which is usually between 20 and 30. Also, in most cities outside of New York the only unions that Off-Broadway producers must work with are actors', musicians', designers' unions and sometimes the directors union.

Many theater companies are nonprofit corporations in terms of their tax structure. This does not mean that the theater cannot make money on a production, but any money the theater does make must go back into the corporation and not to individuals as profit. For this reason all of the employees of a nonprofit theater company, including the producer, are salaried. The money for a production in these types of theaters is raised through ticket sales (including season subscriptions), grants, and donations. In a nonprofit theater there is no investment money because there is no profit to be made.

However, there is a way that non-profit theater companies can get around this and generate income from a profit-making venture. The very successful musical *Hamiton* is a good example of this. It was first produced at the New York Public Theater as a nonprofit production in a small Off-Broadway theater. It was immediately a smash hit. The producers, sensing a potential huge success, formed a profit-making corporation to produce a Broadway production of *Hamilton*. The New York Public Theater was part of this limited partnership so that some of the profit could be funneled back into the nonprofit entity. *Hamilton* has gone on to be a tremendously profitable Broadway success and generated income for its investors and for The New York Public Theater.

Today the producers of Off-Broadway type theater generally create the most interesting union theater going on in the U. S. because they can afford to take more risks with new talent due to the lower production costs. For this reason, the future of theater in America, to a great extent, lies in the theater of Off-Broadway and the resident theater companies throughout the country.

In the 1960's a movement developed in the New York theater which came to be called the *Off-Off Broadway* theater movement. The reasons for this development were three-fold. The first and probably most important reason was the climate of the times. Since theater, like all the arts, reflects what is going on in the society as a whole, the theater of the sixties developed a reactionary wing. This reaction came in the form of structure and ideas. Many of the people involved in this movement were also involved with the counterculture of the 1960's and were opposed to the war in Vietnam. The second reason was a need for a platform to perform and the Broadway and Off-Broadway theater were not open to these new ideas or forms. Third, this new theater movement simply could not afford to produce on Broadway or Off-Broadway because the expense was far beyond the means of these new young artists.

Since there was no place for these new young theater artists to perform, they created their own New York theater spaces. Two of the pioneering spaces were typical of the time and are still typical to some extent. The first, the Cafe Cino, was in a restaurant run by a young poet and playwright named Joe Cino. Cino decided to devote one corner of his small coffee house to short plays and poetry readings. So on weekends short plays that he and some other young playwrights had written would be performed by young actors, and the Off-Off Broadway theater was born. The La Mama Theater followed shortly after in a small loft apartment owned by Ellen Stewart. Cino and Stewart served as producers, gathering plays, directors, designers, and actors together and allowing the plays to happen in their small spaces. Splitting the box office admission total or passing the hat and dividing donations paid all the participants. By the end of the 1960's as many as 100 different Off-Off Broadway theaters were advertising in *The Village Voice.* Their theaters were in cafes and lofts and basements throughout the Greenwich Village area of New York City. No one made much money. Everyone had to have a "day job." But exciting new theater was being performed all over the place.

Today the Off-Off Broadway movement has become an institution of sorts. Actors Equity has an Off-Off Broadway showcase contract. The theater must seat under 100 and the actors must be paid a minimum amount per week for a maximum two-week run. It is still in the Off-Off Broadway theaters that new playwrights, actors, directors, designers, and even producers can get their chance to begin careers. The biggest risks can be taken because the expense is the lowest.

In Washington there are some examples of this type of space and the type of theater company that uses an Off-Off Broadway type theater. The spaces in Washington, D. C. are far more limited than in New York and come and go with some regularity. The most permanent of these companies are Synetic Theater, Spooky Action Theatre and Quotidian Theatre, all of which have their own performance spaces and very stable producing organizations. Theater companies like the Happenstance Theatre, Pointless Theatre and Scena Theatre all of which are ongoing producing entities and production units, which get together to produce just one show, move in and out of various Off-Off Broadway type spaces as their counterparts do in New York and other cities throughout the country. The Off-Off Broadway concept is still alive and well in American theater allowing new ideas and new artists to develop with very little investment and thus very little risk financially. This is a vitally healthy and important element of today's American theater.

Film Business Structure

Like theater, the production of feature films in the United States has been primarily centered in one location. The location has, of course, been Hollywood. This happened primarily because in the beginning days of producing films for the mass audience one needed a great deal of light to expose the film stock on which the films were shot. Sunlight was cheap and constantly available in Southern California. Thus, the major studios were established in Hollywood in the early years of the film industry.

To this day some of those same "major studios" exist and play a principal role in film production and distribution. Each of the major studios (Disney, 20th Century Fox, Paramount, Sony, Universal, Warner Brothers, MGM and Marvel) release and distribute from 15 to 20 films a year. Many of the films that come out of these studios are also produced by them. However, in the film industry today the independent producer plays a key role. *An independent producer is someone who produces a film but is not doing it for one of the major studios.* The studio may agree to distribute the film but first it must be made. In the past few years independent producers have been responsible for well over 60 percent of all the feature films made in the U. S. This is a major difference between film producing today and film producing during the "golden age" of Hollywood in the thirties, forties, and fifties when virtually all films were made by major studios.

The cost of a major studio production versus an independent production can also be greatly different. In 2003 the average production cost of a studio film was between $50-75 million. But many feature films were made in the two to five million dollar range. Obviously, the independent producer cannot afford extravagant special effects and superstars because it is simply too costly. But because the independent producer has less money to lose he can take a few more chances. Thus, many fine films have come from the independents and will continue to as long as they can find a distributor who will handle their films.

Distribution is the key to the financial success of all filmmaking. Without a distributor, a completed film will have very little chance of being seen by a significant number of people and thus is unlikely to make back its investment no matter how small that investment may be. *The **distribution company** is responsible for taking the completed film and leasing it to exhibitors. The **exhibitors** are the people who own the movie theaters in which the audience sees the film.* The distributor has a network of distribution set up so that the exhibitor can know about and preview the films the distributor has available. The distributor will lease the film to the exhibitor, who will pay for the right to show the film in his theaters, or the distributor will set a price for all exhibitors in a given city when a film is not being shown exclusively by one exhibitor.

The advertising costs and the cost of prints of the film are the responsibility of the distributor. Generally speaking the cost of each print of a feature film is between three and five thousand dollars, and a distributor will make as many as two thousand copies for national distribution. The advertising cost of a film is generally around 40 percent to 50 percent of the production cost. So if an average film cost $60 million to make, the distributor will spend as much as $30 million to advertise it, plus the cost of digital copies of he film. All of this cost is up front money and thus high risk. For this reason a distributor gets most of the box office receipts, usually 60 percent to 70 percent in the first few weeks. An example of this can be seen when we look at Paramount Pictures release of *The Godfather, Part III* which opened in 1800 theaters during its first weekend. Exhibitors complained that Paramount demanded that they make a 12-week commitment, with Paramount getting 70 percent of the box office the first two weeks, 60 percent for the following two weeks, and 50 percent for another two weeks.4   Normally a sliding scale would be down to 20 percent or 30 percent after about four weeks. Over a normal 4 to 8 week run of a film the box office split usually equals out to about 50 percent each to the distributor and the exhibitor.

Because the distributor takes his cost off the top from the box office proceeds, a film must make two or three times its production cost at the box office before the producers start to see any of their money. For this reason many times a film that is very expensive will not start to make money until it is distributed to the foreign film markets, television, and the video cassette markets. In the past few years the non theatrical markets have accounted for over 50 percent of the revenue taken in by feature film producers.

In 2014 producers made and released over 500 feature films. These films played on over 38,000 screens throughout the U.S. and Canada, with box office receipts over $10.4 billion dollars and with 2.299 million in tickets sold. But this figure only represents a percentage of the income of a film. In today's market the largest revenue stream can come from the sale and rental of DVD copies of a film and from ecectronic home video, which includes subscription video-on-demand and cable on-demand offerings. This film business network of producers, distributors, and exhibitors is thriving as never before. More people are going to the movies, more movies are being made, and more movie theaters are showing those movies. For the movie audience, the movie business looks healthy and exciting in the twenty–first century.

Television Business Structure

The television business is divided into two basic entities: the broadcast industry, which in 2014 was a $47 billion business and the cable industry, which was a $93 billion business in 2010. One very important thing to understand about the entire television industry, in addition to the fact that it generates huge amounts of income, is that the Federal Communications Commission regulates the industry. This means there are many restrictions on how the industry does business and those regulations are different for each of the two entities. Part of the reason for those differences lies in the manner in which each entity delivers its programming to the public.

. The broadcast network transmits it's programs throughout the country via satellite to the local stations. The television signal is then sent through the air from the local station to the television receiver in our homes. The broadcast networks–ABC, CBS, FOX, NBC, and The CW–are, as we all know, national "commercial" networks. These networks are referred to as "commercial" because they make their money through advertising. The programs of all of these broadcast networks can be seen throughout the country at roughly the same time and in the same nightly sequence anywhere in the U. S. They use what are considered "the public airwaves" to do this. For this and some lesser reasons the FCC deals with the commercial networks in a very restrictive way in terms of what they can produce themselves. The three major networks–ABC, CBS, and NBC–are restricted from producing their own programming by the FCC and thus function primarily as distributors of entertainment programming. This restriction does not, however, apply to the news departments of the three major "commercial networks."

The Public Broadcasting System (PBS) also exists as a "noncommercial" network but uses the same transmission delivery system. PBS derives its operating funds from sources other than advertising and primarily buys programming from television production companies, with the exception of news and public affairs programs.

In much the same manner of the film business, the television industry has production companies that create productions, usually referred to as programs in television. These production companies sell these programs to the commercial networks, to cable networks, or to independent broadcast stations. Many of these companies also produce films.

The networks, both broadcast and cable, function as distributors for the programs. The local stations function as the exhibitors. Generally speaking a local station that is affiliated with a "broadcast network" will carry all of that network's programming. However, the local station will have time slots to fill with other than network programming and will get this from "independent" producers who will either have newly produced programs or "reruns" of old network shows to offer the local station.

In many television market areas, geographic areas of the country served by a group of local television stations, there are more stations than networks. The stations that are not affiliated with a network are called "independent stations" and buy all of the programming that is not produced at the station from independent producers.

The cable networks reach our homes in a much different manner. The network signal is transmitted from a central location by satellite to cable stations throughout the country, which is the same way the broadcast networks function. However, once in the local cable company, the signal is then sent to our homes on a piece of wire called a coaxial cable that is wired into a descrambler box and attached to our television set. The signal can also come directly from the satellite to a receiver dish on our individual home and then wired into a descrambler box and attached to our television set. This delivery system is referred to as "direct satellite cable."

The major difference between cable and broadcast television is the notion of *narrowcasting*. This is quite simply the opposite of *broadcasting*. The *commercial broadcast network* was designed to deliver programs with "mass appeal" to a "broad" spectrum of the population. The *cable networks* focus on a more narrow portion of the audience. So we have cable stations that concentrate on popular music (MTV) or arts programming (BRAVO) or sports (ESPN) or news (CNN). These cable networks tend to produce a great deal of their own programming, which makes them both producer and distributor much of the time. The few things they don't produce for themselves they buy from independent producers.

The local cable company, the *exhibitor*, makes its money through monthly cable charges to each customer and through local advertising. The cable network station, the *distributor*, receives a fee per subscriber from the local cable company and also sells national advertising. The premium channels such as HBO and Showtime simply receive a larger fee for each household because each household is paying more per channel. For this reason the premium channels do not carry commercial advertising.

The newest entity and the broadest and most accessible is the internet. Netflx and Amazon Prime follow the model of a monthly fee and are developing their own content as well as rerunning movies and TV series. But the delivery system is the internet. YouTube has recently become a new content player but is making it's money through advertising. These new internet sources of programming are challenging and changing the older television models and will continue to grow if not dominate in the future.

Producers in the television industry are a bit different from producers of film and theater. In the television industry a producer will have more artistic control than is typical in the other two media. The reason for this is because of the ongoing serial nature of programming television. Since most television programs run for a season or more, there must be one person who maintains the artistic integrity of that series. That person will normally be the executive producer. It is rare that we see one director continually directing episode after episode of a television series. This is partly because of the short time allotted to producing each episode and partly due to tradition within the television industry itself.

As we move toward higher quality television receiving equipment and cable gets into more and more homes, television will probably play a larger role in our viewing lives. For that reason the business of television and the internet will continue to grow and become more and more successful.

The Artist/Craftsman and the Business

There are approximately 377,470 people employed in one way or another in all of show business. Television employs by far the largest number, 150,000, with film coming in second in number of employees and theater third.

Included in that number are the all-important agents that secure work for all manner of show business "talent." The reality is that if you are an actor, director, designer, or writer you probably can't be hired as a "professional," a paid member of one the many artists' unions, unless you have an agent. *Union productions are almost entirely put together by producers working through agents.*

In addition to union productions, there also are nonunion productions in all three media that do often succeed financially and reach an audience of some size. Many independent films are shot as nonunion films or partial union films. In these productions the actors will be members of the Screen Actors Guild (SAG), but none of the rest of the production team will be union. This can also happen in independently produced television to some degree. The major networks and the major film studios produce exclusively union productions. Many films are producing outside the United States to save on production costs and avoid union restrictions. In theater, very often, Off-Broadway and Off-Off Broadway productions will be, to some degree, nonunion productions.

However, being a member of a union for an artist does not guarantee a living from that union. In 2013 Actors Equity, the professional stage actors union, reports of its 45,000 members only 17,500 worked as actors. Of those working members, 38% earned $5,000 or less while only 6% earned $75,000 or greater.

Of course, many actors work in more than one medium and

thus manage to earn quite a good living in that way. Also, some actors make huge salaries often in the several million dollar range. To date in 2016, the highest salary for a single movie is $53 million, which Johnny Debb received to act in the fourth *Pirates of the Caribbean* movie. The highest yearly average is earned by Will Smith who has averaged over $80 million per year for the last several years. But that is rare, as is the three million dollars for Joe Eszterhas's film script for *Basic Instinct*.

In a 2014 report by the New York Department of Labor on the film industry in New York state, the statistics are encouraging for the industry worker. According to this report, New York has 56,000 people actively working in the motion picture industry. The annual average wage in the motion picture industry in New York City was $102,029 in 2013 with the lowest annaul salary at $30,000 and the highest at $150,000. These numbers did not include actor's salaries.

Many artists and craftsmen and women make a very comfortable living in "the business," but to do this one must have both talent and luck. Far more people who want to survive and be "show people" aren't able to do it. It takes an extraordinary amount of luck and talent and a willingness to keep on trying until you make it to be successful as an artist in the business of show business.

The Audience and the Business

We have now looked at how to analyze what we see as audience members. Our relationship as an audience to the business of show business is very clear. If the audience pays to see a production, either by going to the theater and paying the price of admission, or renting the DVD, or buying the products that advertise on television shows, then the producers will continue to produce those types of productions. This means that you should consider carefully what you are willing to support with your dollars and your time.

This book has given you the basis to be a better audience member and/or to continue your growth as a theatre arts artist. Now go out there and spend more time with theater arts that accomplish the dual purpose of art to some degree, be willing to experience a broad spectrum of genres, work at understanding the art and craft of the various artists involved and set a high standard of evaluation that you expect those artist to reach, keep an open mind to new dramatic conventions and styles as they develop within the theater arts, continue to enjoy and explore the exciting worlds created by the theater arts, and effectively explain to others what it is you like and why it is that you like it.

END NOTES

Chapter 1

1. *http://www.statista.com/statistics/252730/leading-film-markets-worldwide--gross-box-office-revenue/*

2. *Joe Brown, Dramatic Discoveries, Washington Post, 7 May 1989. G1.*

3. *Theatre Chat, Theatre Week, 11 January 1988, 52.*

4. *Theatre Chat, Theatre Week, 11 January 1988, 52.*

5. *Rita Kempley, "The Everyday Magic of Bill Forsyth", Washington Post, 15 October 1989.*

6. *Theatre Chat, Theatre Week, 1 February 1988, 52.*

7. *Webster's New Collegiate Dictionary (1979), 916.*

8. *Arts Beat, Washington Post, March 6, 1984*

9. *Alan M. Kriegsman, The Heart of Art in Modern America, Washington Post, 12 March 1989, G1.*

10. *News & Notes, Entertainment Weekly, 23 February 1990, 16.*

11. *Theatre Chat, Theatre Week, 5 December 1988, 72.*

12. *Loring Mandel, "How to Save Television", Parade Magazine, April 3, 1989, 16.*

13. *Byron Belt, "Audience Etiquette", Stagebill, February 1990, 14.*

14. *David Richards, "That Fosse Flair", Washington Post, 27 September 1987.*

15. *Arts Beat, Washington Post, 5 May 1989.*

16. *Theatre Chat, "Julie Taymor: Graven Images", Theatre Week, 26 December 1989, 57.*

17. *Theatre Chat, Theatre Week, 6 June 1988, 72.*

Chapter 2

1.   *Eugene Ionesco, Notes and Counter Notes: Writings on the Theatre (1994), 27.*

2.   *Martin Esslin, The Theatre of the Absurd (1961), xx, 305, 316.*

Chapter 3

1.   *Martin Esslin, The Theatre of the Absurd (1961), 92.*

2.   *Ibid,., 259.*

Chapter 4

1.   *Theatre Chat, Theatre Week, 24 October 1988, 72.*

2.   *Theatre Chat, Theatre Week 15 August 1988, 72.*

3.   *Theatre Chat, Theatre Week 3 October 1988, 72.*

4.   *Theatre Chat, Theatre Week 25 January 1988, 56.*

5.   *Theatre Chat, Theatre Week 28 November 1988, 72.*

6.   *Joe Brown, review of Thin Wall, by Phoef Sutton, Washington Post, 18 October 1985.*

7.   *Paul Hume, " 'Traviata' Travesty: the Violation of Verdi's Violetta", Washington Post, April 7, 1984.*

Chapter 5

1.   *Theatre Chat, Theatre Week, 11 July 1988, 72.*

2.   *Theatre Chat, Theatre Week, 3 October 1988, 72.*

3.   *Theatre Chat, Theatre Week, 6 June 1988, 72.*

4.   *Theatre Chat, Theatre Week, 22 August 1988, 72.*

5.   *Theatre Chat, Theatre Week, 22 August 1988, 72.*

6.   *Theatre Chat, Theatre Week, 25 July 1988, 72.*

7.   *Theatre Chat, Theatre Week, 9 May 1988, 72.*

8.   *Theatre Chat, Theatre Week, 4 April 1988, 44.*

9.   *Theatre Chat, Theatre Week, 6 June 1988, 72.*

10.   *Theatre Chat, Theatre Week, 11 April 1988, 42.*

11.   *Theatre Chat, Theatre Week, 29 August 1988, 72.*

12.   *Theatre Chat, Theatre Week, 26 September 1988, 72.*

13.   *Theatre Chat, Theatre Week, 4 January 1988, 56.*

14.   *Theatre Chat, Theatre Week, 4 April 1988, 44.*

15.   *Theatre Chat, Theatre Week, 10 October 1988, 72.*

16.   *Theatre Chat, Theatre Week, 12 December 1988, 72.*

17.   *Theatre Chat, Theatre Week, 11 January 1988, 52.*

Chapter 6

1.   *Charles Fleming, "Who's the Producer?", American Film, March 1990, 12.*

2.   *David Denby, "An Epic Masterpiece Revisited", Premiere, February 1989, 27-28.*

3.   *David Richards, "Arms & the Men", Washington Post, April 6, 1989.*

4.   *Richard Harrington, "Performers on the Job", Washington Post, May 5., 1992.*

5.   *Neil O. Alper et.al., Artists in the Work Place, (1996), 5, 6.*

REFERENCED FILMS

Alien (20th Century Fox, 1979) Director: Ridley Scott. Screenplay: Dan O'Bannon.

Basic Instinct (Carolco, 1992) Director: Paul Verhoeven. Screenplay: Joe Eszterhas.

Batman (Warner Bros., 1989) Director: Tim Burton. Screenplay: Sam Hamm & Warren Skaaren.

Brazil (Universal, 1985) Director: Terry Gilliam. Screenplay: Terry Gilliam & Tom Stoppard.

Casualties of War (Columbia, 1989) Director: Brian DePalma. Screenplay: David Rabe.

Dangerous Liaisons (Warner Bros., 1988) Director: Stephen Frears. Screenplay: Christopher Hampton, based on his play and the novel "Les Liaisons Dangereuses" by Choderlos de Laclos.

Dick Tracy (Touchstone, 1990) Director: Warren Beatty. Screenplay: Jim Cash & Jack Epps Jr.

Die Hard (20th Century Fox, 1988) Director: John McTiernan. Screenplay: Jeb Stuart & Steven E. de Souza, based on the novel "Nothing Lasts Forever" by Roderick Thorp.

Dr. Jekyll and Mr. Hyde (MGM, 1941) Director: Victor Fleming. Screenplay: John Lee Mahin, based on the novel "The Strange Case of Dr. Jekyll and Mr. Hyde" by Robert Louis Stevenson.

Dr. Strangelove or How I Learned to Stop Worrying and Love the Bomb (Columbia, 1964) Director: Stanley Kubrick. Screenplay: Stanley Kubrick, Peter George & Terry Southern, based on the novel "Red Alert" by Peter George.

Do the Right Thing (Universal, 1989) Director & Screenplay: Spike Lee

Driving Miss Daisy (Warner Bros., 1989) Director: Bruce Beresford. Screenplay: Alfred Uhry, based on his play.

Fatal Attraction (Paramount, 1987) Director: Adrian Lyne. Screenplay:

James Dearden.

Four Weddings and a Funeral (Polygram, 1994) Director: Mike Newell. Screenplay: Richard Curtis.

The Godfather, Part III (Paramount, 1990) Director: Francis Ford Coppola. Screenplay: Mario Puzo & Francis Ford Coppola.

Gremlins (Warners Bros., 1984) Director: Joe Dante. Screenplay: Chris Columbus.

King Kong (RKO, 1933) Directors: Merian C. Cooper & Ernest B. Schoedsack. Screenplay: James Creelman & Ruth Rose.

The Last Boy Scout (Warner Bros., 1991) Director: Tony Scott. Screenplay: Shane Black.

Lawrence of Arabia (Columbia, 1962) Director: David Lean. Screenplay: Robert Bolt.

Monty Python and the Holy Grail (Columbia, 1975) Directors: Terry Gilliam & Terry Jones. Screenplay: Graham Chapman, John Cleese, Terry Gilliam, Eric Idle, Terry Jones & Michael Palin.

Moonstruck (MGM, 1987) Director: Norman Jewison. Screenplay: John Patrick Shanley.

Pretty Woman (Touchstone, 1990) Director: Garry Marshall. Screenplay: J.F. Lawton.

Pulp Fiction (Miramax, 1994) Director: Quentin Tarantino. Screenplay: Quentin Tarantino & Roger Roberts Avery.

Rain Man (MGM, 1988) Director: Barry Levinson. Screenplay: Ronald Bass.

sex, lies and videotape (Columbia, 1989) Director & Screenplay: Steven Soderberg.

Soap Opera (Ol' Black Bear Productions, 1992) Director: Perry Schwartz, based on the play by Ralph Pape.

Star Wars (20th Century Fox, 1977) Director & Screenplay: George Lucas.

Superman: The Movie (Warner Bros., 1978) Director: Richard Donner. Screenplay: Mario Puzo, Robert Benton & David Newman.

The Taming of the Shrew (Columbia, 1967) Director & Screenplay: Franco Zeffirelli, based on the play by William Shakespeare.

Terms of Endearment (Paramount, 1983) Director & Screenplay: James L. Brooks, based on the novel by Larry McMurtry.

Titanic (Paramont, 1997) Director: & Writer: James Cameron.

2001: A Space Odyssey (MGM, 1968) Director: Stanley Kubrick. Screenplay: Arthur C. Clarke & Stanley Kubrick, based on the story "The Sentinel" by Arthur C. Clarke.

The Untouchables (Paramount, 1987) Director: Brian DePalma. Screenplay: David Mamet.

Varsity Blues (Paramount, 1999) Director: Brian Robbins. Screenplay: W. Peter Iliff.

When Harry Met Sally (Columbia, 1989) Director: Rob Reiner. Screenplay: Nora Ephron.

Wings of Desire (Orion, 1988) Director: Wim Wenders. Screenplay: Wim Wenders & Peter Handke.

Yellow Submarine (United Artists, 1968) Directors: George Duning & Dick Emery. Screenplay: Erich Segal.

REFERENCED PLAYS

Cats (Harcourt, Brace, Jovanovick, 1983) by Andrew Lloyd Webber.

The Caucasian Chalk Circle (Arcade Publishing, Inc, 1995) by Bertold Brecht

The Cherry Orchard (Cambridge University Press, 1996) by Anton Chekov

A Chorus Line (Applause Theatre Books Publishers, 1995) by Marvin Hamlisch & Ralph Burns

Coming Attractions (Samuel French, Inc. 1983) by Ted Tally

Death of a Salesman (Viking Press, 1949) by Arthur Miller

A Doll's House (Dramatists Play Service, 1998) by Henrik Ibsen

Driving Miss Daisy (Dramatists Play Service, 1987) by Alfred Uhry

Endgame (Grove-Atltic, 1983) by Samuel Beckett

Equus (Viking Penguin, 1984) by Peter Shaffer

Frankie and Johnny in the Clair de Lune (Dramatists Play Service, 1988) by Terrance McNally

Ghosts (Dover, 1997) by Henrik Ibsen

Hair (Dover, 1970) by James Rado

Les Liaisons Dangereuses (Faber & Faber, 1985) by Christopher Hampton, based on the novel by Choderlos de Laclos.

Lysistrata (R, Dee, 1991) by Aristophanes

MacBeth (Bantam, 1988) by William Shakespeare

MacBett (Grove Press, 1973) by Eugene Ionesco

A Midsummer Night's Dream (Bantam, 1988) by William Shakespeare

Les Miserables (Dover, 1980) by Andrew Lloyd Weber

Mother Courage (Grove-Atltic, 1987) by Bertold Brecht

Oedipus the King (University of Massachusetts Press, 1982   ) by Sophocles

Oh Dad, Poor Dad, Momma's Hung You in the Closet and I'm Feelin' So Sad (Hill and Wang, 1958) by Arthur Kopit

The Phantom of the Opera (Dover 1986) by Andrew Lloyd Webber & Charles Hart

The Second Shepherd's Play (Simon and Schuster, 1966) Anounymous.

A Soldier's Play (Nelson Doubleday, 19821) by Charles Fuller

The Spanish Tragedy (St. Martin Press, 1995) by Thomas Kyd

Starlight Express (Dover 1989) Andrew Lloyd Weber.

Thin Wall (Grove, 1982) by Phoef Sutton

The Three Penny Opera (Grove-Atltic, 1983) by Kurt Weill & Bertold Brecht

The Three Sisters (Grove, 1953) by Anton Chekov

La Traviata (Dover, 1990) by Giuseppe Verdi

Waiting for Godot (Grove-Atltic. 1987) by Samuel Beckett

The World of Sholem Aleichem (grove, 1954) A. Singer,

REFERENCED TELEVISION SERIES

ER (NBC)

That 70's Show (FOX)

The Flintstones (ABC)

The Gary Shandling Show (HBO)

The Honeymooners (CBS)

Married with Children (Fox)

Masterpiece Theatre (PBS)

Moonlighting (ABC)

NYPD Blue (ABC)

Three's Company (ABC)